Hockey Stories
On and Off the Ice

Other books by
Dan Diamond and Associates

Total Hockey: The Official Encyclopedia
of the National Hockey League

The NHL Guide & Record Book

Toronto Blue Jays
25th Anniversary Commemorative Book

Hockey Stories
On and Off the Ice

**Dan Diamond and James Duplacey
with Eric Zweig**

**Andrews McMeel
Publishing**

Kansas City

01 02 03 04 05 RDH 10 9 8 7 6 5 4 3 2 1

Library of Congress Cataloging-in-Publication Data

Diamond, Dan.
    Hockey stories on and off the ice / Dan Diamond and James Duplacey.
        p. cm.
    ISBN 0-7407-1903-3 (pbk.)
      1. Hockey—Anecdotes. I. Duplacey, James. II. Title.

GV847 .D52 2001
796.962—dc21

                2001035871

Book design and composition by Just Your Type

*For everyone who
cares for the game*

Hockey is like a disease. You really can't shake it.
Former NHL goaltender Ken Wreggett

INTRODUCTION

Ice hockey is a sport unlike any other. No other professional game generates such a combination of speed and artistic motion. Still, the success of the sport is dependent on one other factor—its intense physical contact. Contact breeds contempt. Contempt breeds conflict, conflict breeds interaction, and interaction leads to confrontation. And confrontation is the major element that makes the game exciting. From on-ice jousting to gamesmanship to one-upmanship, the "meeting of the muscle" between athletes of this caliber, competing at full speed and top volume, can only result in attitude, action, and reaction. And that creates the hype and hyperbole that produce the tall tales, both true and false, that make hockey more than just a game.

To examine the passion and the pain of this game, you need to gain a perspective into the game's earliest recruits and famous old coots, back when King Clancy was a prince, Eddie Shore took no nonsense, and Howie Morenz was the heart of the Canadiens. To appreciate the power of the hockey player as a cultural and athletic icon, you need only look into the eyes of Rocket Richard and read the words of the players, fans, and politicians who idolized him. And, of course, the game of hockey has always been enriched with "character" players, those lovable loons who are as quick with the quip as they are with their fists. Their words are here as well.

Hockey is a man's game. The team with the most real men wins.
Brian Burke, general manager of the Vancouver Canucks

Along the way, we'll visit the ice palaces, rinks, arenas, and barns where the sport is played. We'll pop on down to the minor leagues, where icons and myths, both real and imagined, were created. It was the bus leagues that helped make names like Ned Brady, the Hanson Brothers, Billy Goldthorpe, Harry Neal, John Brophy, Harry Sinden, and even Bob Costas famous.

Call them pros, call them mercenaries—but in fact they are just grown up kids who have learned on the frozen creek and flooded corner lot that hockey is the greatest thrill of them all.
Lester Patrick, architect of the PCHA and a Hall-of-Fame player, coach, and manager

All photos used in this book are from the collection of Dan Diamond and Associates, unless otherwise noted.

How the West Was Won

Tall Tales Along the Hockey Trails of the West Coast

My Wife and Artificial Ice

The only developments in hockey over the last 25 years for which the Patricks cannot take credit is the introduction of the moan and groan and the six-man game.

Elmer Ferguson, *Montreal Star* sportswriter

Shortly after Lester Patrick was married in Victoria, British Columbia, on March 7, 1911, he and his new bride left for a honeymoon trip to Boston. By more than just coincidence, the happy couple arrived in the Massachusetts seaport at the same time that the Montreal Wanderers and Ottawa Senators were in town to play a two-game exhibition series. Patrick renewed acquaintances with a host of former teammates and opponents and even picked up $100 for refereeing the two contests. Most important to Lester Patrick, the matches were being played at the Boston Arena, one of the few artificial ice palaces in operation at that time.

Lester and his brother Frank had decided to form and operate a rival hockey league in western Canada, which eventually would be dubbed the Pacific Coast Hockey Association. They realized they could not count on hockey weather in the damp climate of British Columbia

Lester Patrick

and the surrounding Pacific Northwest. To make their dream of a West Coast league a reality, they needed to find an alternative way to make and sustain safe and sturdy ice, despite the conditions.

While he was in Boston, Lester gathered a great deal of technical information about the installation and maintenance of artificial ice. With the information Lester collected on his honeymoon trip, the Patrick brothers were able to conceive and construct Canada's first two artificial ice rinks—the 10,000-seat Denman Arena in Vancouver and the 4,000-seat Willows Arena in Victoria. When both were completed in December 1911, the Patricks were able to launch their new league by January 1912. Soon, the entire face of professional hockey would be dramatically changed.

You Can't Expect Him to Remember Everything!

The Patricks not only played the game brilliantly, they legislated it into modernism.

Elmer Ferguson, *Montreal Star*

Talk about wearing different hats! In addition to founding the PCHA, Lester and Frank Patrick also served as owners, managers, coaches, and players in Victoria and Vancouver respectively. By the 1913–14 season, the third year of the loop's existence, Frank had also added the title of league president to his résumé. So, it shouldn't come as a surprise that he decided to cut back on his own ice time when the 1914–15 season rolled around. In fact, he didn't suit up for his first game until February 12. Well, it quickly became evident that Frank was spending too much time in the boardroom. When he hit the ice to take his first shift of the season, he fell flat on his face, much to the delight of the Victoria crowd! It seems in his haste to make a dramatic entry, he forgot to remove his skate guards.

When Is a Canary Just a Pigeon?

In the fall of 1916, the Canadian government expropriated the Willows Arena in Victoria so it could serve as a military installation to train troops preparing to embark for Europe to fight in the First World War. The Victoria club was relocated to Spokane, Washington, and coined the Canaries, because of their yellow uniforms. After a one-year stay in the cage and a last-place finish, the team flew the coop, never to return. The PCHA did return a franchise to Victoria when the conflict overseas ended and the arena was once again preparing for games instead of war.

The Other Stanley Cup Story of 1919

The Seattle Metropolitans of the Pacific Coast Hockey Association became the first American-based team to win the Stanley Cup by defeating the Montreal Canadiens in the 1917 championship finals. The star of the series was a hot-shot sniper named Bernie Morris, who was coming off a season that had seen him score a career-high 37 goals in just 24 games and lead the PCHA in scoring with 54 points. Morris went on to score a remarkable 14 goals in only four games against the Habs, including a double hat trick in a 9–1 pounding that decided the series. Morris had another fine season in 1918–19, finishing second in the PCHA in goals (22) and points (29). Yet when the Metropolitans met up with Montreal for a Stanley Cup rematch later that season, he was no longer in the lineup.

For years, armchair historians wondered what had happened to the Seattle superstar. There was never any mention of him in most of the historical accounts of the series, since much of the attention was focused on the great flu epidemic that caused the death of Montreal rearguard Joe Hall and the hospitalization of numerous other players. Most historians assumed that Morris had fallen ill like so many of his comrades. But that was not the case. Bernie Morris was not ill, injured, or inept. He was incarcerated. It turns out that Morris had been arrested by government authorities of the United States for failing to report to the U.S. Army and evading the draft.

Morris was a Canadian citizen, but he was employed in the United States. Therefore, he was registered under the military service act in both countries. Originally, he had been given a military exemption by the governments in Canada and the United States, but somehow his status had been reversed in the USA. Not that Bernie knew all this. Like every other athlete of this era, Morris couldn't afford not to work after the hockey season ended. So, he had taken an off-season job working in the woods of northern British Columbia, and the draft notice sent to him in November 1918 was never forwarded to him. This wasn't a rare occurrence in the fall of 1918 and the early winter of 1919. With the Spanish influenza epidemic raging, not too many mail couriers were willing to trek deep into the woods to what was probably an unsafe and unsanitary lumber camp just to deliver a piece of mail.

So, when Morris didn't report as ordered in his draft notice, the authorities assumed he was a draft dodger and he was arrested. On April 12, 1919, Morris was convicted of being a deserter by the U.S. Army and subjected to a general court-martial at Camp Lewis in Tacoma, Washington. He was sentenced to two years at hard labor at the most foul of all penal institutions, the island of Alcatraz outside the city of San Francisco.

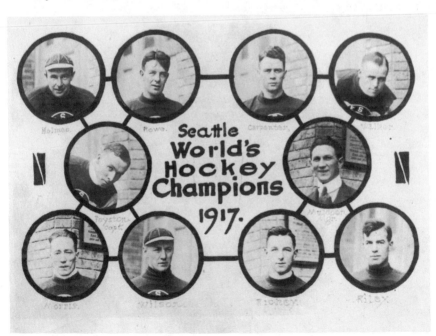

1917 Seattle Metropolitans

The original Stanley Cup

When PCHA president Frank Patrick heard of Morris's predicament, he vowed he would fight the case right to the desk of the president of the United States if he had to. The Canadian government also got involved. Although there isn't any evidence to suggest Morris ever really went to the big house in Alcatraz, it was almost a full year before he was finally exonerated. He missed the entire 1919–20 season but was allowed to return to action in time to suit up for Seattle's 1920 Stanley Cup series against the Ottawa Senators. Morris went on to play ten more seasons in the PCHA, the Western Canada Hockey League, minor pro leagues, and the NHL.

Will This Thing Ever End?

T he NHL and the PCHA were facing some new kids on the block when the 1921–22 season rolled around. A new concoction called the Western Canada Hockey League had been formed and the league's directors informed the "old boys" they intended to challenge for the Stanley Cup. With teams based in Edmonton (the Eskimos), Regina (the Capitals), Calgary (the Tigers), and Saskatoon (the Sheiks), the new loop seemed to be standing on solid ground. As the season chugged toward the conclusion of its initial campaign, only the Saskatoon club was hopelessly out of playoff contention. In fact, when the schedule ended on February 27, Edmonton and Regina had identical records of 14–9–1 with Calgary merely a half step off stride with 14 wins and 10 losses.

The playoff format of the day in the PCHA, the NHL, and the new Western League called for the first-place team to meet the second-place team for the championship. In order to determine who had finished first, Edmonton and Regina agreed to replay a game that had ended in a stalemate on March 1. The result was a surprising 11–2 romp by the Eskimos, giving them sole possession of first place, thanks to their now revised record of 15 wins and 9 losses. Regina had slipped a cog and now stood tied with Calgary at 14–10. Those clubs were then ordered to play a two-game, total-goal series to determine the second-place finisher. The Capitals won the lid-lifter of the series 1–0 on March 2 and finished off the set with a 1–1 tie the following evening to take the series two goals to one.

That series victory gave the Capitals the opportunity to right a wrong and face their rivals from Edmonton again. However, considering that this would be Regina's fourth game in as many nights, the team's chances didn't appear to be promising. Bullet Joe Simpson gave the Eskimos an early lead, but Dick Irvin tied the score for Regina and the game ended in a 1–1 saw-off. After a well-earned day of rest, the Capitals turned the tables on the Eskimos and froze them out of further postseason play with a 2–1 victory on March 6.

There wouldn't be any time for the Caps to rest on their laurels; in fact there would be no time to do anything but pack up, suit up, and get back on the ice. The Regina players spent the one off day they had on the train, traveling to Vancouver, where the well-rested PCHA champion Vancouver Millionaires were waiting for them. The series began on March 8, and once again Dick Irvin was the hero as the Caps squeezed out a 2–1 victory. It was the team's sixth game in eight nights. The club then had two full days to convalesce before playing the final part of the two-game, total-goal series. This time, the Capitals found that their gas tanks were empty, their legs were weary, and their offensive spark was exhausted. Vancouver sailed to an easy 4–0 victory to take the series five goals to two. Some scribes mused that perhaps it was just as well the Capitals lost. If they had won the series, they would have immediately boarded another train and traveled halfway across the country to meet the Toronto St. Pats in the Stanley Cup finals. But you can take it to the bank that there wasn't a single player on that Regina squad who wouldn't have been willing to give it a try.

Sometimes a Change Is as Good as a Rest

When the Seattle franchise withdrew from the PCHA before the opening of the 1924–25 season, the PCHA's two remaining teams—Vancouver and Victoria—decided to join the Western Canada Hockey League. Though the lay of the land at that time still called for a team's six best players to remain on the ice for as much of the game as possible, Lester Patrick began experimenting with a new system. Since his lineup had been augmented by a group of former Seattle players, he had power in numbers. Patrick found that he could now ice a second unit of players that was almost as good as his first line. The Silver Fox began mixing and matching his lines and even tried changing players while the play was still going on. The Cougars not only claimed the WCHL title that season but they were also able to defeat the vaunted Montreal Canadiens in the Stanley Cup championship series. By using multiple lines and quick changes, Patrick was able to keep his troops fresh, while the Canadiens were still dependent on just one main offensive unit, the high-flying line of Howie Morenz, Aurel Joliat, and Billy Boucher. The Habs' trio was run ragged by Patrick's prancing princes and as a result, the Cougars became the last non-NHL team to win the Stanley Cup.

The On-Ice Arbitrators

Although we don't often like to admit it, the game of hockey would be impossible to play without the presence of an on-ice arbitrator. In fact, referees have been just as important to the development of the game as any of the boardroom builders who believe they are the ones who shaped the sport.

Let's begin at the very beginning. The game of hockey starts when the referee blows his whistle and drops the puck at center ice. And for the most part, it's always been that way. But there have been subtle changes along the way. As any referee from the turn of the century would have said, take my whistle, please.

A Waitress and a Waghorne

When the game was in its infancy, referees used steel whistles to signal starts and stops in play. Since these were the only kind of whistles available at the time, the refs really had little choice. But they wished they had. Before the introduction of artificial ice machines, rinks were kept as cold as the air outside, causing the steel whistles to freeze. When this occurred, as it invariably did, two things happened: the whistle wouldn't blow properly, which often led to blows from angered players and fans who were convinced the ref had missed an obvious foul or goal. And, second, those frozen peace pipes would stick to the ref's lips and tear away a healthy layer of skin every time the arbitrator removed it from his mouth.

It took a pioneering referee named Fred Waghorne to solve the problem. Old Fred was in Kingston, Ontario, preparing to handle a game in the Queen City. As he stepped into the lounge of his hotel, a waitress ambled out of the dining room and rang a dinner bell to signal that supper was being served. That gave the clever and creative Waghorne an idea. He borrowed the bell from the hotel—after giving a generous tip to the young waitress, we assume—and he used it that night instead of the stoic whistle. Everyone loved this novel idea. Not only did it allow the ref to stop play quickly, it helped accelerate the pace of the game. Years later, when heated arenas became common, the whistle was reintroduced. But when hockey was in diapers, it was the bell that drew a crowd.

Another innovation that can be traced directly back to Mr. Waghorne is the method of conducting a face-off. In the earliest days of the game, the referee would place the puck on the ice and yell, "Play." That was the cue for the centermen to begin slashing, slicing, and dicing with their sticks in a vain attempt to gain possession of the loose disk. More often than not, the ref would come away from that confrontation with a bloody shin and a battered toe. That wasn't the only complication. Rarely was the "draw" cleanly done, and the whole procedure would have to be repeated.

Waghorne solved that dilemma, but it took a rare moment of anger for him to generate the basis of the idea that would change the game forever. One evening in 1900, Waghorne was refereeing a game in Southern Ontario—even he was unsure of the exact location although he did nail it down to either Brantford, Paris, or London. "I was being hammered on the legs and feet at every draw," he remembered. "I was getting fed up and I guess I blew my top a little. I said to myself, 'To heck with the rules in this case!' I told the centermen what I was going to do. They were to place their blades on the ice about a foot or two apart, and I'd stand back and toss the puck between their sticks. After the rubber hit the ice, they could do as they darn well pleased. It worked out so well there wasn't a single squawk from the players or the fans." Soon, the new innovation was being practiced throughout the province and within months, it was universally accepted.

Even Referees Pay the Price

The End of the Storey

One of the legendary figures in Canadian sports is Red Storey, a record-setting football player and one of the most trusted and honored referees ever to adjudicate a game of ice hockey. However, even his on-ice judgment was questioned, and it cost the NHL one of its more colorful characters.

The incident in question occurred during game six of the 1959 Stanley Cup semifinals between the Montreal Canadiens and Chicago Blackhawks. The Hawks were making their first playoff appearance in many years and referee Storey had his hands full controlling the game on the ice while ignoring the catcalls of the raucous fans. Already at odds with Storey for a couple of earlier non-calls, the crowd erupted in anger when he failed to call a penalty on Montreal's Albert "Junior" Langlois after he flattened Bobby Hull late in the third period of a 4–4 tie. Storey felt the hit was clean, although the other 20,000 arbitrators in attendance didn't agree with him. As the fans screamed and the Blackhawks steamed, Montreal's Claude Provost calmly picked up a loose puck, skated in on netminder Glenn Hall, and coolly drilled the puck past him. That goal stood as the winning tally, giving the Habs a 5–4 win in the game and a four-games-to-two victory in the series.

When the final horn sounded, a couple of unruly and well-lubricated fans jumped the restraining barrier in an attempt to show Storey the error of his ways. Montreal defenseman Doug Harvey came to the official's aid, warding off the fans with his stick and escorting Storey to safety. After the game, league president Clarence Campbell admitted to a reporter that he thought Storey "froze" on a couple of his non-calls. When the exasperated referee was unable to receive an apology from Campbell, the future Hall-of-Fame referee resigned and never again worked as an official in an NHL game. "When you don't have the support of your superiors," Storey said at the time, "it is time to quit."

The irony of the situation is that Storey was not supposed to be working that game. Chicago coach Rudy Pilous made a special request that the veteran whistle-tooter be brought in for that match because he "was the best there was" at handling tough games in tight situations.

Toe Blake and Jacques Plante

The $2,000 Sock

Asimilar fate brought the career of referee Dalton McArthur to an end two years later. Only this time it was for a penalty that was called and it was Montreal that was on the receiving end in a game against Chicago. The Canadiens, who were searching for a sixth consecutive Stanley Cup victory and a record 11th straight trip to the finals, were engaged in a furious battle for their playoff lives.

With the series knotted at one game apiece, the two teams battled through three periods of regulation time and another two full 20-minute overtime sessions without a winner being declared. Nerves were getting frayed, tempers were getting hot, and the players were getting steamed. Montreal had to kill off four straight penalties in overtime alone, while the Blackhawks skated through the first 40 minutes of extra time penalty-free.

Midway through the third overtime frame, McArthur thumbed Dickie Moore off for tripping, setting up the Hawks' fifth overtime power play. Less than a minute after Moore went into the box, Chicago's Murray Balfour scored to give the Hawks the win and a 2–1 lead in the series. Shortly after Balfour "lit the lamp," Montreal bench boss Toe Blake jumped onto the ice surface, went up to referee McArthur, and walloped him squarely on the nose. How Blake managed to avoid suspension is a mystery that armchair scribes still like to debate about. He did receive a hefty fine, however, in what the newspapers described as "Toe's $2,000 sock." McArthur's punishment was more subtle but more substantial. His contract was not renewed and he never refereed in the NHL again.

A Simple Twist of Fate

Another referee who fell under the disciplinary knife was a one-time Eastern Amateur League star turned whistle-blower named Mel Harwood. It was Harwood's fate to be the referee during game four of the 1942 Stanley Cup final series between Toronto and Detroit. The Red Wings were in full control of the series when the fourth contest began. The Motowners had easily won the first three games of the series and were expected to wrap up the title that evening. However, the Leafs had other plans. Coach Hap Day made a pair of bold roster moves, benching Gordie Drillon and Bucko McDonald, two of the club's top veterans, and replacing them with raw rookies. After a scoreless first period, the Wings built a 2–0 advantage before the Leafs squared the affair at 2–2, heading into the final frame. Carl Liscombe's 35-footer eluded Leaf goaltender Turk Broda less than five minutes

1942 Toronto Maple Leafs

into the third stanza, giving the Wings a margin no one expected they would squander.

Only mere moments after Liscombe's marker had given Detroit the lead, referee Harwood nailed Red Wing forward Alex Motter for a tripping infraction. Seconds later, Leafs captain Syl Apps potted the tying goal, which was followed in due course by a 12-footer off the blade of Nick Metz that put the Leafs on top for the first time. With only 69 ticks remaining on the clock, an irate Red Wings fan tossed a hot water bag in the direction of linesman Sammy Babcock. Detroit's Eddie Wares picked it up and handed it to Harwood. If it was intended to be a joke, the referee didn't get it. Harwood, tired of the bickering and bantering he heard every time he skated past the Detroit bench, thumbed Wares to the box with a 10-minute misconduct. Wares refused to comply, which earned the Detroit team a too-many-men-on-the-ice penalty. Well, all hell broke loose. Fans littered the ice with debris and the players started swarming Harwood like piranhas. When the final whistle blew, Detroit coach Jolly Jack Adams flew onto the ice and slugged the referee before his players could restrain him. NHL president Frank Calder called Adams onto the carpet and put him on ice—so to speak—for the rest of the finals. Adams was suspended and Ebbie Goodfellow took over behind the bench.

The Leafs went on to become the only team in pro sports history to win a best-of-seven championship series after losing the first three contests. Harwood never refereed in the NHL again, but he did gain some fame as the first head coach of the Coast Guard Clippers, a legendary wartime squad that played in the old Eastern Hockey League.

Junior Langlois, Don McKenney, and Doug Harvey

The Last Line of Defense

Goaltenders are three sandwiches shy of a picnic. From the moment primitive man lurched erect, he survived on the principle that when something hard and potentially lethal comes toward you at great velocity, you get the hell out of its path.

Jim Taylor, sports columnist

While the thrill of hockey rests mostly in its speed and offensive wizardry, most pundits admit the game is won by playing airtight defense. The most important rung in that ladder is the goaltender, the hulking creature who stands alone like a prisoner in his own 6 x 4-foot cage, resembling an alien from a foreign land. But the goalie is also the last line of defense, and his performance determines the thin line between victory and defeat.

No position in the game has changed more over the years, both in the equipment used and the way the position is played, than that of the goaltender. In the primitive years of the game, goalies wore the same equipment as the other players. Protection didn't seem to be all that important anyway. When the game was still in its development stage, no one could raise the puck. Then, a crafty player discovered that if the puck was released using the backhand part of the blade, you could really loft the thing. While the players were overjoyed, the goalies were just annoyed. Clearly, new innovations were necessary.

Still, it wasn't until a goaltender from Winnipeg named Whitey Merritt showed up wearing cricket pads to protect his legs that the idea of goalie pads was introduced. Soon, goalies were improvising all kinds of innovations, from adding a wedge of lumber to their sticks to making the handle wider to wearing a belly protector like the ones used by catchers in baseball. Not that life between the pipes was any easier.

Larry Hillman (2), Johnny Bower (goalie), and Stan Mikita (21)

Until 1917, goalies weren't even allowed to drop to their knees to make a save. They were forced to stand erect and use only their feet, hands, and every other part of their anatomy to stop the puck from entering the net. And this only added to the slow pace of those early games.

Praying Benny

Playing goal is like being shot at.

Jacques Plante, Hall-of-Fame goaltender

The most innovative goaltender in the first decade of the NHL was Clint Benedict. He just wouldn't accept the rules as written. Benedict invented all kinds of ploys and ruses that allowed him to leave his feet to make a save, and all seemed to fall within the limited confines of the rules. He would pretend to slip and fall, stopping the puck at the same time.

One of his most popular techniques was falling to his knees in mock prayer when a player skated in on him alone. Of course, while he was praying to the heavens, he was also thwarting the breakaway. Fans took to calling him "Praying Benny."

Soon, every goaltender was copying Benedict's style and finally the legislators gave in and allowed goalies to leave their feet. It was a double-edged sword, however. The closer you got to the ice, the more often the puck could strike you at an unprotected part of the body, and the most glaringly open area was the face. If Benny wanted to see the action up close and personal, he was going to have to take a few stitches for the team.

On the night of January 7, 1930, Benedict was tending goal for the Montreal Maroons in a game against their inter-city rivals, the Montreal Canadiens. During the game, the great Habs forward Howie Morenz sped into the Maroons zone and unloaded a blast from about 25 feet out that Benedict didn't see until the last second. It hit the goalie in the head and, in the words of a local reporter, "crushed in the side of Benny's face like an eggshell." Benny had taken a dozen shots like this one, but this was the first time he was conked cold long enough that he

Clint Benedict in goalie gear in Montreal

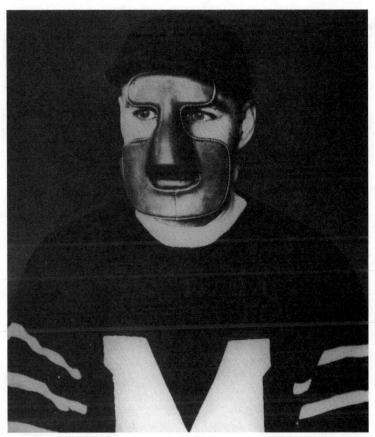

Clint Benedict in his mask

didn't come to until he was already in the hospital. A quick inspection in the mirror confirmed his fears. His nose resembled a mashed melon and his blackened eyes made him appear to be more raccoon than human being. It would be six weeks before Benny was able, willing, and stable enough to resume tending goal in the NHL.

Jacques Plante in his first mask

The First Mask

We start out with goalies wearing masks. Every club has a defenseman or two who goes down to smother shots. Soon, they'll want masks. All forwards will wear helmets. The teams will become faceless, headless robots, all of whom look alike to the spectators. We can't afford to take that fan appeal away from hockey.

**New York Rangers general manager Muzz Patrick
on the future of hockey, 1959**

When Benedict decided he was ready to face live action again, he wasn't going to go out there alone. He needed an ally. So, Benny did what any other man would do in this situation. He invented the goalie mask. Now, I know what you're going to say. Everybody knows that Jacques Plante invented the goalie mask. Well, that's only partially true. Plante was the first goalie to wear the mask regularly, game in and game out. However, the first crease-cop to step into the corded cottage wearing a mask, primitive as it was, was Clint Benedict.

There is some confusion over exactly what kind of mask Benedict wore. The Hockey Hall of Fame has a photograph of him wearing a leather contraption, while other scribes of the times remember him modeling a mask that resembled the headgear a boxer wears in his sparring matches. What isn't lost in the sands of time is the result of Benedict's date with destiny. On the night he wore his facial protection, the Maroons lost 2–1 and Benny blamed the mask. "The nosepiece protruded too far," he recalled. "It obscured my vision on low shots."

As for Mr. Plante, he continued to wear the mask because the Canadiens continued to win. The Habs went on a lengthy winning streak

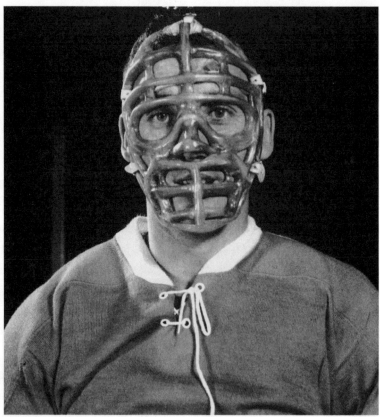

Plante's fiberglass "skeleton" mask became his trademark through the early 1960s.

after Plante first took to wearing the mask on that night after Halloween in 1959. Except for one game that he played without the mask shortly after introducing it, Plante never again played without facial protection. He went on to model, make, and create new masks for himself and other NHL goaltenders for the remainder of his lengthy career.

The Aftermath

Stressful? Do you know a lot of jobs where every time you make a mistake, a red light goes off over your head and 15,000 people start booing?

Hall-of-Fame goaltender Jacques Plante

Many armchair historians still like to ponder the question, "What if the Habs had lost when Plante first pulled on the mask? How long would it have been before the mask became a reality?" Well, the question is moot. Even by the beginning of the 1966–67 season, a full seven years later, the mask was still not an accepted piece of gear in most goaltenders' equipment bags. Even in the last season of that mystical era known as the "Original Six," all six starting goaltenders—Detroit's Crozier, Chicago's Hall, Toronto's Bower, Montreal's Worsley, New York's Giacomin, and Boston's Johnston—were still facing slap-shooting, banana-bladed blasters like Wharram, Hull, and Mikita with their bare faces. Most of the teams' "second" goalies that year did wear the mask and each was still considered to be nothing more than a backup goalie. That should tell you all you need to know about the "old-school" coaches and general managers of the era.

I've told you guys before, goalies don't think.

Detroit goaltender Chris Osgood when asked what he thinks about when Wayne Gretzky has a clear breakaway on him

Hey, I've Been Here Before!

When Lester Patrick made his now infamous appearance in goal during game two of the 1928 Stanley Cup finals, most fans and scribes assumed that the 44-year-old New York Rangers coach and manager hadn't suited up in anger for years. Certainly, no one would have expected that the Silver Fox had ever taken a place between the pipes. Well, Lester Patrick was a pretty smooth operator and he'd never let the facts get in the way of a good story. But the truth was that not only had Patrick played an entire season on defense with the Victoria Cougars just two seasons earlier at the age of 42, he had also made an emergency appearance in goal with the team during the 1921–22 season.

The Innovators

What are they going to want up there next, a bucket of chicken?
**Edmonton Oilers general manager Glen Sather
upon seeing a water bottle on the net for the first time**

First goaltenders to wear a face mask after Clint Benedict:

Jacques Plante, Montreal Canadiens, November 1, 1959
(Montreal 3, New York Rangers 1)

Don Simmons, Boston Bruins, December 13, 1959
(New York Rangers 4, Boston 3)

Emile Francis, Spokane Comets, December 17, 1959
(Seattle 4, Spokane 3)

Gil Mayer, Cleveland Barons, December 30, 1959
(Rochester 2, Cleveland 2)

First game in which three goaltenders were used:

Toronto 3, New York Rangers 3, April 2, 1966
Johnny Bower (1st period, nine shots, eight saves)
Terry Sawchuk (2nd period, 14 shots, 13 saves)
Bruce Gamble (3rd period, 10 shots, nine saves)

First goaltender to wear goalie pads stuffed with horsehair made famous
by Hamilton, Ontario, harness and leather shop owner Pop Kenesky:

Jake Forbes of the Hamilton Tigers, 1922–23

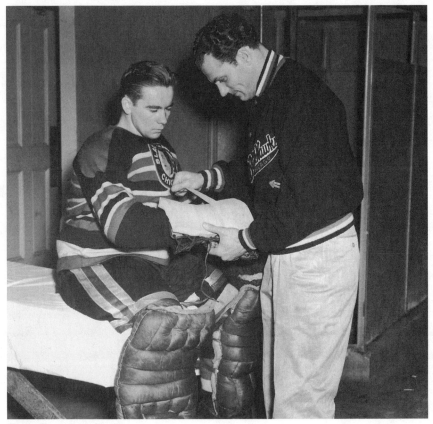

Emile Francis and trainer

First goaltender to fashion a "trapper" glove for his catching hand by putting an added cuff on a first baseman's mitt:

Emile "Cat" Francis, Chicago Blackhawks, 1947–48

Along the Blueline

When I came to the Rangers, I wanted to be a defenseman,
but nobody would chip in for an operation to have half my brain
removed!

Goaltender Bob Froese—April 1987

Up front, you don't have to think as much. That should help Dave.

New York Rangers forward Don Maloney, after his brother
Dave was switched from defense to forward

Half the game is mental, the other half is being mental.

Former Maple Leafs defenseman turned broadcaster
Jim McKenney

I was a fringe player. I was the kind of guy who, if I didn't look
good getting on the plane, I got sent down.

Former New York Islanders coach Bill Stewart, on his
talents as a defenseman

Except for a brief time during the roaring 1970s and the expansion-weakened 1980s when blueliners were often frontliners on the statistical sheet, the role of the defenseman in hockey has not changed all that dramatically. Even in the formative years, defenders were big-boned bruisers, content to stay at home in their own zone and hammer any unsuspecting forward who dared roam into their kitchen. Defensemen weren't expected to lug the puck up the ice—that would have to wait until Eddie Shore came on the scene in the late 1920s. And they certainly weren't expected to score a goal.

Dick Irvin, the legendary bench boss who won Stanley Cup titles with both the Toronto Maple Leafs and Montreal Canadiens, remembered the first time he ever heard of a defenseman scoring a goal. When the Winnipeg Vics journeyed to Montreal to play the Wanderers for the Stanley Cup in January of 1900, Irvin was still a youngster with a deep love for his city, his team, and his game. In those days, it was commonplace for crowds to gather outside the telegraph office and

Dick Irvin

read the reports of the game as they were being transmitted across the wires. "I remember the commotion—almost bewilderment—in the crowd that night," the elder Irvin recalled, "when word was flashed that Rod Flett had scored a goal. Flett was a defenseman; they were supposed to stay on the job in their own end of the ice. A defenseman who could carry the puck and score a goal? No, it just wasn't done."

Only later did the facts present themselves. Flett had lifted a long backhand shot that went high into the rafters. There were numerous banners hanging from the ceiling of the arena and the opposing goaltender lost sight of the puck as it disappeared among the flags. When it came down, it landed right in front of the goaltender and rolled untouched into the net. Flett had scored the first recorded goal by a defenseman in the history of the Stanley Cup challenge series.

The Characters

In the 1920s and 1930s, the NHL was blessed by having two of the most colorful characters ever to don the blades playing in the league at the same time. One was a crafty Irish-blooded leprechaun from Ottawa named Frank "King" Clancy, a wee tyke with a heart of gold, a chin of steel, a twinkle in his eye, and a glorious gift of gab. The other was Eddie Shore, a rough and ready farm boy who had studied agriculture at college until the lure of the ice grabbed him. Together, he and Clancy would create an on-ice universe of their own, a world full of tall tales that teetered on the laughable ledge of lunacy.

Clancy started his career with the Ottawa Senators in 1921, but it didn't take long for him to become the subject of legend and lore. The Stanley Cup finals of 1923 matched the western champion Edmonton Eskimos against Clancy's Ottawa Senators. The Sens were not given much chance of bringing the silver chalice back to the nation's capital because they were decimated with injuries. Four of the team's top players, Lionel Hitchman, Eddie Gerard, George Boucher, and Harry Helman, were all sidelined suffering from one malaise or another.

The Senators headed out west with only eight players, including the baby-faced Clancy, who was only in his second semester as an NHL regular. Because of their depleted roster, the players who were capable of suiting up were forced to play out of position and in every position. Clancy himself lined up at defense, forward, and rover in one game. But even the ready-for-anything Clancy never expected to have to take a turn in the nets. Yet that's exactly what occurred.

In game four of the series, Senators' goaltender Clint Benedict was penalized for slashing Eskimos' forward Duke Keats. In those days, if the goalie did the crime, he also did the time, and Benny was admonished to the sin bin. When this occurred, a player had to stand in for the goalie, without the benefit of so much as a goalie stick.

So, who should be the first to volunteer to take his place? Why, the crafty Clancy, that's who! Tommy "Tay-Pay" Gorman, the man behind the Senators' bench that evening, mulled over Clancy's offer and decided to accept it. After all, he reasoned, that would probably be the best place for him. Clancy took Benedict's place between the pipes and the Senators threw up a defensive wall in front of him. Try as they might, the Edmonton squad couldn't seem to break through the barrier.

Just when it appeared the situation was well in hand, Clancy decided to provide a little drama. Though he had strict instructions to stay glued to the cage, when Clancy spied a loose puck in front of the net, the devil got the best of him. He scampered out of the net, grabbed the loose disk and started a mad dash up the ice. "I was frantically yelling, 'Get back, get back,'" remembered Tommy Gorman, "but I should have saved my breath. Clancy skated right up to Edmonton's defensemen, pulled one out of position, then contented himself by firing a long shot right on goal. Grinning happily, he scooted back to his own end of the rink." Not only did Clancy become the first position player to play nets and not to allow a goal in Stanley Cup competition, he also became the first goalie to record a shot on net. A legend was born.

Eddie Shore

The Gift of Gab

*I socked Eddie once as he was getting to his feet and skated
like mad to the other side of the rink.*

King Clancy on how he "beat up" Eddie Shore

Part of the Clancy legend rests solely on the righteous rhetoric that
only an Irishman like Clancy could produce. In fact, the Toronto Maple
Leafs once won a playoff series because Clancy was able to get so far
under the skin of his adversary, the entire flux and flow of the series
was altered.

To the hockey purist, the beauty of this entire saga resides in the
fact that Clancy didn't pull the wool over the eyes of some unfortunate
busher who was unaware of Clancy's powers of persuasion. No, the
legend lives because Clancy nailed Eddie Shore, and it was the great
Boston rearguard who sank the Bruins' ship with his loose lips.

*It was pretty much a 50-50 proposition. You socked the other
guy and the other guy socked you.*

Eddie Shore

If there was any player in the NHL who should have been willing,
ready, and able to resist a classic Clancy commentary, it was Eddie
Shore. He'd seen and heard them all before. But even he was powerless
when put under the spell of a classic Clancy chicanery.

In March 1936, the Maple Leafs and Shore's Boston Bruins were
engaged in a two-game, total-goal series. In the opening match of
the set, the Beantowners had outhustled the aging Leafs and had
skated to a convincing 4–1 victory. Shore and the Bruins carried that
seemingly secure three-goal bulge into the second and final game. With

King Clancy

the Bruins up 1–0 in the second period, Shore took a penalty and the Leafs stormed the Boston net, potting a pair of goals to give them a 2–1 lead in the game and pulling them within a pair of goals of tying the series.

The referee of this affair was Odie Cleghorn, who had stretched the rules to their extremes when he was a player. He and Shore had met many times on and off the ice, and their relationship was a cool one. After he returned from the box, Shore watched in amazement as Charlie Conacher, the Leafs' powerful rightwinger, decked two or three Bruin skaters without any penalty being called. Later, the Big Bomber clocked Shore himself and once again referee Cleghorn's whistle stayed in his pocket.

Clancy knew the moment was now ripe for rebate. As they lined up for a face-off, Clancy whispered in Shore's direction, "That bloody Cleghorn's blind as a bat, Eddie. He's robbing you sure as hell. Conacher had to go for that vicious hit on you." Shore glanced over at Clancy, but the King kept his eyes pointed down toward the ice surface. Eddie shook his head in bewilderment. Where did those inspiring words come from? In the end, it didn't matter. They were manna from heaven, as far as Shore was concerned, and he was going to treat them as gospel.

Before Cleghorn could even drop the disk, Shore was in his face, berating him for his poor conduct as a referee. Cleghorn, confused but resolute, listened to Shore's bleating and calmly warned the Bruins' rearguard to return to his position or he'd have no other choice but to force him to cool his hot temper in the sin bin. When Shore refused to comply with this order, Cleghorn thumbed him off the ice for a two-minute stay in penalty box purgatory. As the referee skated away to report the infraction to the timekeeper, Shore retrieved the puck and fired a low and accurate shot that plunked off referee Cleghorn's backside. Odie wheeled around and informed Mr. Shore that the penalty box would now be his one and only home for an additional 10 minutes.

Clancy and Imlach

The arbitrator's ruling was final and that spelled disaster for the Boston boys. In those days, the guilty party spent the entire term of his sentence in the box. That meant the opposing team could fill the net with as many pucks as they could shoot past the goaltender until the sentence had been served. As the Bruins' best player cooled his heels and his hot collar, the Leafs exploded for a quartet of goals and captured the series by a total score of 8–6. One could say Shore had the last laugh when the Leafs failed to win the Stanley Cup that spring, but then again, Eddie Shore never laughed at anything.

It's been said that Clancy started a hundred fights and never finished one. Well, if that's true then Shore started a hundred fights and finished every one.

One More for the King

During the 1960s, King Clancy was Punch Imlach's most trusted confidant. It wasn't rare for Imlach to hand the reins of the team to the King for a game or two so Imlach could watch the game from the press box and chart breakout plays and special team setups. But most of the time, Imlach had the King on curfew duty, doing room checks when the team was on the road.

On one particular evening, he stopped off at a room, knocked on the hotel door, and waited for an answer. When the player asked who was there, King replied, "It's just Clancy here, checking to make sure you're all tucked in for the night." Well, the player answered in a rather incredulous tone, suggesting he was insulted to think that Mr. Clancy would even question his moral fortitude. The player opened the hotel room door, and just as he did, he noticed that the King's eyes were nearly bulging out of his head. It seems the player had a "guest" for the night, and she just happened to wander out of the washroom wearing nothing but a smile.

When the King's head had cleared, he politely asked the young man—referring to the undressed damsel—"Ah, now, could you tell me who that is?" With a completely straight face, the player answered, "King, I've never seen her before in my life."

Some years later, Clancy was asked why he didn't report finding the bare but beautiful lady in that player's room to Coach Imlach. After some careful thought, the King replied, "Well, it's not like she was in the buff, you know, she was wearing earrings!"

Doug Harvey

Hungry Like the Wolf

One of the great defensemen and characters of all time was the Montreal Canadiens' Norris Trophy–winning wizard, Doug Harvey. There are still people out there who swear this yarn is true. In the early 1960s, the Sudbury Wolves were a powerhouse senior team on the northern Ontario circuit and an Allan Cup favorite, year-in and year-out. The club was also one the first teams anywhere to have a mascot, years before every team on earth adopted the tradition. After every Sudbury goal, a fellow in a wolf suit would run from one side of the arena to the other while the crowd howled like banshees in wolf's clothing.

In the early 1960s, the Montreal Canadiens journeyed to Sudbury to play a preseason exhibition game to give the northern fans an opportunity to see some big-name NHL players playing right there under their noses. Toward the end of the match, with the Habs holding a more-than-comfortable margin in goals, Doug Harvey purposely put the puck into his own net. When he returned to the bench, he was greeted with a scowl from Coach Toe Blake, who never liked to give up a goal regardless of the score or the circumstances. Harvey peeked up at his bench boss and said, "Sorry, Toe, but you've got to admit that it was worth it, just to see that wolf."

Howie Morenz

Forwards Ho!

The Babe Ruth of Hockey

You know, Howie Morenz won't be remembered as a two-way player, and that's all wrong. He went in terrific bounds, his skates seldom seemed to touch the ice. He flashed from the net to the blueline faster than I can say the word 'blueline.'"

Conn Smythe, the builder of the Toronto Maple Leafs

When the NHL was first starting to gain notoriety in the United States, much of the sizzle that sold the steak was based on the popularity of Howie Morenz, the Montreal Canadiens' swift-skating superstar and a man revered as a God in hockey-mad Quebec. In the USA, Morenz was called "the Babe Ruth of hockey" not only because every rink would be full when he came to town but because the spectators knew they were going to see something special occur on the ice surface that evening.

Morenz, who could skate as fast backward as he could forward, was a phenom, before the word was even invented. He would go on to reinvent the way the game was played, and there wasn't a team or player on the planet who could touch him when he was in his prime.

Ironically, the team that had the most trouble with Morenz was the team that signed him, the Canadiens. Four NHL clubs were vying for his services while he was still a teenager, but only one was going to be able to get his signature on the dotted line. Leo Dandurand, the coach and manager of the Montreal Canadiens, sent Cecil Hart—a close friend and ally—to Stratford with a pair of signed, but blank, checks with instructions to sign the kid, no matter what it cost. It worked.

On July 7, 1923, Hart convinced Morenz to sign a three-year contract worth $3,500 a year, with moderate increases each season. Since Morenz was still a minor, the deal had to be cosigned by his father.

Six weeks later, Dandurand received a letter in the mail from Morenz, returning both the money and the contract. The letter explained that he wasn't going to be able to meet the terms of the deal, and he would like to stay home in Stratford. Dandurand immediately fired off a train ticket and a demand that the young man make his way to Montreal to meet with him the following day. After some tough talking from Dandy Dandurand—which included the advice that a contract signed must also be a contract honored—Morenz broke down in tears and admitted that he felt he wasn't good enough to make the Canadiens' team. Dandurand told the youngster to report to training camp, and if the rest of the players and coaches felt he was a wash, he would be given a ticket back home on the spot, no questions asked.

Well, as it turns out, Morenz was brilliant in camp, and not only did he make the team, he was given a spot on the Habs' top line. He was a force from his first NHL game and never looked back. Now, this story has been told numerous times, so its details are fairly common knowledge. What often hasn't been told is the caveat that Dandurand presented Morenz midway through his rookie season. "I called him into my office," Dandurand recalled, "and I told him his three-year contract would be destroyed. His new contract would cover only one season, so that when he came of age, he would be eligible to negotiate his own deal, under his own terms. Howie was happy and contented. He was being treated like a man. There was no weeping in my office that day. Neither of us were in the mood."

He's clean, fair, and sportsmanlike, and he always gives his best. Add his bullet shot to his speed, and you have, in my mind, the greatest offensive combination in hockey today.

Eddie Shore, heaping praise on Howie Morenz, which he rarely did for anybody—at any time

This Too Shall Pass

The 1910–11 National Hockey Association season was quite a romp for the Ottawa Senators. They forged an impressive 13–3 win-loss record, crushed a pair of opponents (Galt and Port Arthur) in two Stanley Cup challenge matches, and observed their top star, Marty Walsh, score 48 goals in just 18 league and playoff games. Following the campaign, club secretary Martin Rosenthal told reporters that he believed the publication of goal-scoring statistics was hurting teamwork. Mr. Rosenthal said he believed the problem could be overcome by the presentation of a trophy to the NHA player with the most assists. Many observers felt his plan was a worthy one until one astute fellow pointed out that the NHA did not record assists. Well, the delegation said, let's start. That only created a further complication. No one could agree on the method of determining how assists should be calculated. It wasn't until the second season of the NHL, in 1918–19, that "official" assist records were kept.

9/9/99

O ver the course of the past 60 years of NHL history, three men have done more to define the sport of hockey than any other athletes to play the game—Maurice Richard, Gordie Howe, and Wayne Gretzky. This trio shared a common bond of talent, desire, tenacity, dedication, and courage. They were born to win and would pay any consequence to see their team skate to victory. And though on the surface, it may appear trivial, they also shared another bond. They wore the same numbers.

Every kid growing up in Canada wanted to wear #9. And it was because of these three athletes—The Terrific Trifecta—that the game of hockey has been able to endure.

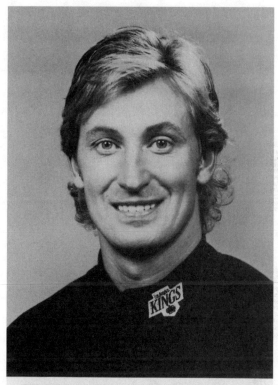

WAYNE GRETZKY
Forward

Gretzky as an NHL rookie, 1979

THE GREAT ONE

Gretzky on Gretzky

Now, Gordie Howe, he's my kind of player. He had so many tricks around the net, it's no wonder he scored so many goals. I'd like to be just like him. And if I couldn't play hockey I'd like to play baseball with the Oakland Athletics and Vida Blue.

Wayne Gretzky in his first ever interview, 1971

Nobody plays better defense on me than Kasper. When I got married I half expected to see Kasper standing at the altar in a tux.

Wayne Gretzky on super-pest and super-shadow Steve Kasper

Eight days ago, we were the toast of the town. Eight days later we're Thanksgiving turkeys.

Gretzky on the plight of the Los Angeles Kings

He brings something special. I don't know what it is, but if you ask him, you couldn't understand his answer.

Gretzky on Ranger forward Esa Tikkanen

Gretzky as a member of the Los Angeles Kings

Even to this day, some people question my ability. It's beneficial that I have to prove myself every night. It motivates me more than anything.

Wayne Gretzky, 1987

You'll always miss 100 percent of the shots you do not take.

Wayne Gretzky

Some people skate to the puck. I skate to where the puck is going to be.

Wayne Gretzky

All the Rest Talking About the Best

I marveled before how he did things but playing with him, I got to see things differently. I'll give you an example. We were in Buffalo and Wayne was behind the net with the puck. I was coming in from the wing and I thought, darn, he's missed the chance to pass. It was amazing. Through all those skates, sticks and legs, the puck just came right through and all I had to do was shoot it. More amazing was the pass just floated through, not hard at all. I can't explain it. Somebody said he has eyes all over the rink. So, what's the secret then? I don't think there are words to describe how he does the things he does even if I could understand how he does them.

Former Edmonton Oilers teammate Willy Lidstrom

When this skinny teenager named Gretzky began unveiling his hockey genius with the Edmonton Oilers 20 years ago, it became apparent he was playing the game of hockey on a level somewhat different from everyone else.

Lidstrom again

He's the master at it. It seems every record he's broken has been like that. We should feel happy for him for doing it, but right now I'm finding it difficult. It's just a killer. This was a huge game for us in terms of winning. And he comes along with 53 seconds left.

Current Oilers coach Craig McTavish on the night #99 broke Gordie Howe's all-time points record

He's so skinny he could fit in a McDonald's straw!
Writer on the young Wayne Gretzky

The only way you can check Gretzky is to hit him when he is standing still during the national anthem.
Former Boston general manager Harry Sinden

Some guys play hockey. Gretzky plays 40 mile-an-hour chess.
Lowell Cohn, sports journalist

Gretzky was also the catalyst for the NHL's presence in Texas, Arizona, Florida, Tennessee, areas never previously considered as hockey markets. In the process, he became a megastar away from the arena; people who knew little of hockey knew the name Gretzky. He is a modern day Mr. Hockey, succeeding Gordie Howe, his idol, in carrying that title so gracefully.

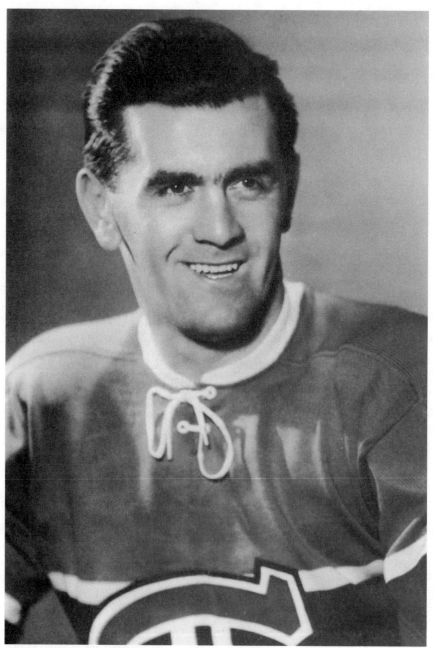

Maurice "Rocket" Richard

The Rocket: Maurice Richard

When Maurice "Rocket" Richard died on May 27, 2000, the province of Quebec stood still for three days while athletes, politicians, historians, and common folk tried to put into perspective what he meant to his province, his sport, and his country. Here is a sampling of some of those thoughts.

There wasn't a dry eye in the house when he received a standing ovation at the closing of the Montreal Forum. It was extremely moving; I almost fell to the ground, my knees were trembling so hard.

Ronald Corey, former Montreal Canadiens president

Goal scoring for Richard was basic and elemental, less an act of skill and more an act of will. His eyes told the story. Piercing like bullets, dark, almost maniacally wide and askew, their focus was somewhere else. Not on a puck, not on a camera, not on any opponent in his way; around, through, and beyond all of them; focused on what only need and desire could see. His were dangerous eyes, disturbing, disturbed, not to be reasoned with, capable of anything, frightening to friend and foe. Beyond control. His eyes mirrored a soul that had to get to the net.

Ken Dryden, writing in *Time* magazine

What set the Rocket apart was his intensity. If we were down a goal or two, "the Rocket" was there to tie it up again. As soon as he would touch the puck, you could feel the electricity in the crowd. It was amazing to see how people would react, not only in Montreal, but everywhere he played. There's never been another like him.

Former teammate and fellow Hall-of-Fame member Bernie "Boom Boom" Geoffrion

We all wanted to wear #9 when we were kids, not just me. This man played a role in my career through the pride he displayed each time he wore the sweater of the Montreal Canadiens.

Guy Lafleur

He was one of the best players who ever played in the history of hockey. He was a man who had a lot of respect in the hockey world.

Mario Lemieux

I have a theory: Whenever he scored a goal the cheer at the Forum was just a decibel higher than when anybody else scored, no matter the importance.

Dick Irvin, Jr., hockey broadcaster and author

He was an icon in Montreal, in Quebec. People just worshiped him, so did we all.

Dickie Moore, former teammate

He had a solid will to win and was a tireless worker. Skilled and determined, he was in all respects an indispensable teammate but also a formidable opponent.

Lucien Bouchard, former Premier of the Province of Quebec

He'd walk into a room and it was like a king walked in. I lived in Three Rivers and the people in Quebec, they loved him, they absolutely loved the guy. He was a great guy.

Don Cherry

What truly set him apart was his extraordinary intensity. He played with great emotion and flair and possessed an unmatched will to win. His dazzling combination of skill and drive not only made him one of the greatest hockey players ever, it also made him a symbol to all of what it takes to be a true champion.

Jean Chrétien, Prime Minister of Canada

He was to become an icon, a legend. He was, in every way, one of a kind.

Red Fisher, senior journalist for the *Montreal Gazette*

Dickie Moore, who played with the Rocket during the Fabulous Fifties, when the Canadiens reached the Stanley Cup finals in 10 straight seasons, remembers some of the hostile turns the crowd would take when the Rocket was really stirring the pot. One night they were sitting side by side on the bench when a clanking sound startled Moore. He looked around, and lying on the floor behind him was a large metal object. "I looked at Rock and said, 'Do you know what that is?' And he said no. So I told him, 'It's a hammer, it would've killed either one of us, and I've got a pretty good idea it wasn't aimed at me!'"

Many pundits have speculated just exactly how the Rocket was pegged with his explosive nickname. Former teammate Ray Getliffe has as good a description as any. "I'm not sure, but I think the name came up in his second year," recalled Getliffe. "I was on the bench and he got the puck at the blueline, deked two guys, and streaked in with that fire in his eyes to score. I said, 'Geez, he went in like a rocket.' A sportswriter overheard me, you know, and the nickname stuck like glue."

Gordie Howe

And Howe

Not many fans remember or even realize that Gordie Howe was ambidextrous and could fire the puck with equal velocity both right-handed and left-handed. Jack Adams, the longtime manager of the Detroit Red Wings, was one of the first to recognize this unusual trait in his young protégé.

The shy youngster from Floral, Saskatchewan, by way of Saskatoon had already had a go-round with the New York Rangers, but he was so homesick he left camp before Lester Patrick, the Rangers' top hound, could get a decent look at him.

A year later, Howe was skating with a group of wanna-be's in a Detroit Red Wings tryout. "I saw this one big kid skate in on the net and shoot right-handed," Adams recalled years after the fact. "Back he came on his next rush and he had to move out of position on his wing. But he got the puck and fired another shot left-handed. I sat up and really took notice when that happened. I hadn't seen anything like that in years."

Adams called the kid over to the boards, and they had a conversation. Ultimately, Adams signed the busher and the legend was on its way to being born.

They should have two pucks on the ice when he's out there. One for him and one for the rest of the players.

Toronto coach Hap Day

Claude Lemieux (32)

Iᴛ's Pᴜɢɪʟɪsᴍ Nᴏᴛ Pᴏᴇᴛʀʏ

Tough Guys Talk Tough

I grabbed it and squeezed it back into place. It gave a little crunch and popped right in.

New York Rangers tough guy Jay Wells, on how he fixed his broken nose

That's so when I forget how to spell my name, I can still find my #$%@& clothes!

Chicago Blackhawks enforcer Stu Grimson, on why he keeps a photo of himself above his locker

I'd rather fight than score.

Dave "The Hammer" Schultz

If I play badly, I'll pick a fight in the third period, just to get into a fight. Afterward I can say, "Yeah, I sucked, but I won the fight, didn't I?"

Former Bruins bad boy Derek Sanderson

When you're playing, you can always go out and punch somebody when you get frustrated. You can't do that now.

Bob Plager, speaking about "Life After Hockey"

I didn't stick the landing. I fell to the left when my pelvis broke. The Swedish judge only gave me a 9.8, but the U.S. and Canadian judges both gave me a 10.0.

Tony Twist after he miraculously lived following a serious motorcycle accident

What are you, the fight doctor now or something? You've never been in a fight in your life, so what are you talking about?

Buffalo tough guy Rob Ray's reply to a reporter after being pummeled by Edmonton's Georges Laraque

They will do a lot of talking, but I'm not sure they will understand each other.

Detroit's Darren McCarty on teammate Vladimir Konstantinov shadowing Devils' forward Claude Lemieux

Cornelius. That's what we like to call him. Man, he gets under your skin. A real Planet of the Apes *guy. I mean, look at him. Seriously. He looks like Cornelius.*

Matthew Barnaby's take on Lyle Odelein of the New Jersey Devils

We go back and forth. Keith's got a pretty good endorsement deal with Jack in the Box. That's pretty much him, that giant pumpkin on his head.

Matthew Barnaby on former Phoenix forward Keith Tkachuk

If he had anything more than air in his head, he may have.

Former bruiser Chris Nilan commenting on whether a head butt he received courtesy of Al Secord had hurt him

The penalty box was kind of a gross place to go. Guys have been in there bleeding and stuff. No one's cleaned the place since 1938.

Dave "Tiger" Williams, the NHL's all-time leader in penalty minutes

I was low on sticks and didn't want to lose one on his head.

Mike Richter, on not swinging at Tie Domi, who had sucker-punched Richter's teammate Ulf Samuelsson

Even a blind dog finds a bone once in a while.

Noted enforcer Kelly Chase, after scoring twice in an NHL game

All my friends back home fight on the street and all they get is arrested.

Patrick Cote, on earning his salary with his fists

The Montreal Victorias. The Stanley Cup is just a silver punch bowl in this photo. To the right of the Cup is the senior amateur championship trophy.

THE HISTORIC BATTLES FOR LORD STANLEY'S SILVER CHALICE

Vics versus Vics: The 1899 Controversy

The whole thing began with two clubs with the same name volleying the Stanley Cup back and forth like a badminton bird. And it ended with the referee just packing up and taking his puck home. In between, there was intrigue, mystery, threats, compromise, and deceit. And it's still only 1899!

The Montreal Victorias first became Stanley Cup champions in 1895. In February 1896, they were dethroned by another band of Victorias who called Winnipeg, Manitoba, their home. The Montreal version of the Vics regained their grip on Lord Stanley's silverware in December, and they were still champions when the Winnipeg Victorias challenged them again in February 1899. By this time, the teams knew each other very well, which helped fuel the first great controversy in Stanley Cup history.

The 1899 challenge series opened on February 15. Winnipeg went ahead early in the game on a goal by Tony Gingras and was still clinging to that slim margin with less then two minutes to play. But Bob McDougall tied the score, setting the stage for Graham Drinkwater's last-second heroics. With only seconds left on the clock, Drinkwater grabbed the puck, negotiated his way through the entire Winnipeg team, and potted the winning goal just as the buzzer was about to sound. That's hockey!

The excitement of game one whipped up unprecedented interest for the second encounter of the series, which was scheduled to take place three nights later. Ticket speculators made a killing—and a profit—as a crowd of nearly 8,000 fans crammed their way into the Montreal Arena for the Saturday night affair. Despite poor ice conditions caused by the unseasonably mild weather, the teams did not disappoint the sold-out throng. The match was a tightly played, hard-hitting affair that saw the home side nursing a 3–2 lead with only a few minutes left to play. It was then that the trouble began.

Pushing hard for the tying goal, Winnipeg's Tony Gingras elbowed his way past Montreal's Bob McDougall, only to receive a wicked slash across the back of his leg for his efforts. Referee Bill Findlay sent McDougall off for a three-minute rest in the sin bin, but the Winnipeggers were incensed that such a light sentence was imposed for such a hard slash. To accentuate their displeasure at the referee's call, the Vics decided to retreat to their dressing room as a sign of protest. As they departed, they made sure they directed some very uncomplimentary remarks at referee Findlay.

Findlay, who felt his integrity and judgment had been insulted, left the scene and abruptly went home. A search party had to be formed and sent out to find the referee and convince him to return to the rink. When he finally arrived back at the arena some 65 minutes later, Findlay gave the Winnipeg players 15 minutes to suit up and continue the game. But the Vics reiterated their position on the matter: they would not return to the ice unless McDougall was banished for the rest of the game. Findlay refused to meet the Winnipeg demand and the westerners refused to alter their stand. So, when the 15-minute deadline expired, Findlay awarded the game, and the series, to Montreal.

An elaborately inscribed hockey stick that was used in this first great Stanley Cup controversy can still be seen today at the Hockey Hall of Fame in Toronto. Dated February 18, 1899, it tells the story of that night's game, including a smug remark that seems to sum up the sordid affair: "Fizzy the Referee went home."

Kenora versus Brandon: The Forgotten Series of 1907

It's a fairly well-known piece of hockey lore that the Kenora Thistles hailed from the smallest town to ever wrap its arms around the Stanley Cup. There were only 4,000 souls living in Kenora—give or take a few prospective inhabitants—at the time they captured their title. It's also common knowledge among Stanley Cup purists that the Thistles had the shortest reign of any chalice champions, winning the Cup in January and losing it in a rematch against the Montreal Wanderers in late March. Most students of hockey history are aware that the rematch of 1907 was clouded in all kinds of murky controversy but only the most ardent of silverware surveyors know there was actually another Stanley Cup series that was played before the rematch ever took place. This is that story.

Kenora has always had a rich hockey heritage. When the community was still known as Rat Portage, the Thistles captured the Manitoba and Northwest Hockey League title in 1903 and challenged the Ottawa Silver Seven for the Stanley Cup. Although they lost to the powerhouse squad from the nation's capital, they continued to ice winning teams, thanks to a forceful foursome of local lads named Tommy Phillips, Si Griffis, Billy McGimsie, and Tom Hooper. In 1904–5, they once again issued a challenge to the Silver Seven for possession of Lord Stanley's mighty mug and once again they were defeated.

After winning another league title in 1905–6, the Thistles made their third attempt to wrestle the Cup from the eastern powerhouses. Only this time, they brought in some extra firepower, adding both Art Ross and Joe Hall from the Brandon club. The Thistles' challenge had to be delayed until another series between Ottawa and the Montreal Wanderers was completed. When the Wanderers dethroned the Silver

Seven in a major upset, they had to prepare to defend their new title against Kenora in January 1907. The Thistles, bolstered by the addition of Ross (Hall was suspended and unable to play), knocked Montreal off their Stanley Cup perch by sweeping the best-of-three affair with 4–2 and 8–6 victories.

Although they had lost the Stanley Cup to Kenora, the Wanderers went on to finish first in the Eastern Canada league and then promptly issued another challenge to the Thistles. When they did, they requested that acting Stanley Cup trustee William Foran forbid any outside players being added to the Thistles roster. They also asked that the Thistles be forced to accept the challenge immediately.

Trustee Foran thought it was rather rude of the Wanderers to think they could bully their way into an instant appointment with the holders of the Stanley Cup, so he ruled that any challenge by Montreal would have to wait until the end of the Manitoba hockey season. But he did

The 1907 Montreal Wanderers

agree with the Wanderers' stand on the use of outside players. It was decided that any player who was a member of a team in the same league as the challenger would be ruled ineligible to play in defense of the Cup. In other words: no ringers from Manitoba would be allowed.

Now this presented the Thistles with a serious problem. The new ruling made Art Ross unavailable and they had already lost Billy McGimsie to an eventual career-ending shoulder injury. If the team were going to have any hopes at all of defeating the Wanderers, they would need outside help. Since players from their home province were out-of-bounds, the Thistles infiltrated the neighboring province of Ontario and grabbed former Ottawa Silver Seven stars Alf Smith and Rat Westwick for their defense of the Cup.

However, Foran announced that these players wouldn't be allowed to participate either. Well, this opened a whole new nest of snakes. The adding of out-of-province talent was a common practice, and Foran's ruling brought howls of protests from across the hockey-mad land.

"On every occasion in which [Montreal and Ottawa] defended the Cup," wrote the *Kenora Miner*, "they had players from outside their own club. Smith and Westwick will have played three games (for the Thistles) before a Stanley Cup challenge is met. They are certainly as much entitled to play with Kenora as the majority of the men the Wanderers are bringing up to play with them."

Even the *Toronto Telegram* agreed: "William Foran . . . declares that Smith and Westwick are not regular members of the Kenora team and will not be allowed to defend the silverware. But if not, why not? Is Hod Stuart, who helped the Wanderers against Kenora in Montreal, a legitimate member of the Wanderers or of Pittsburgh, with whom he played during the early part of the season? Does [Pud] Glass legitimately belong to the Wanderers or to Montreal [AAA]? He certainly contracted to play for the latter."

For his part, Foran told reporters in Ottawa that "two wrongs have never yet made a right, though one would think so from the stand taken by some of the critics of my action." He added that in the past, the trustees "made it a point never to interfere in the affairs of teams playing for the Stanley Cup unless compelled to do so by a protest from one or other of the teams concerned. Such a protest was never made regarding the eligibility of players until the present instance. If a protest had been made against Ross or Stuart in January, it would have been sustained."

Foran's arguments may have swayed votes in a court of law, but he could not win in the court of public opinion. "He may be a silver-tongued orator," said the *Winnipeg Tribune,* "but it will take more than oratory to convince [people] that the Thistles are getting a square deal

The 1906–7 Kenora Thistles

in the present controversy." As the *Telegram* stated: "It has been a case of everything goes in professional hockey, and at this late date it is hardly likely the whole situation can be changed by a few words from the ever-ready Mr. Foran."

Meanwhile, as the issue of player eligibility was debated in the papers, another problem appeared. The Wanderers wanted the Stanley Cup games to be played in Winnipeg, where the city's larger rink would ensure greater gate receipts. However, the Thistles felt their fans deserved to see the games on their home ice and Foran agreed.

It was during this dispute that a member of the Thistles management is said to have taken the Stanley Cup down to the dock and threatened to throw it into the Lake of the Woods. In the end, the two teams were able to settle their disputes. The Wanderers agreed to let Kenora use Westwick and Smith, while the Thistles agreed to stage the games at the Winnipeg Arena in late March.

Apparently lost in the controversy over the eligibility of players and the location of the games was William Foran's other ruling: that Kenora could not defend the Stanley Cup until the championship of the Manitoba league had been decided. Foran's ruling meant only one thing: the champions of the Manitoba league would be considered Stanley Cup champions and as such, they must be ready to withstand a challenge to that status against the Montreal Wanderers.

So, logic tells us, if a team other than Kenora were to win the Manitoba title, they would be deemed Stanley Cup champions and the Cup would be theirs to defend. As it turns out, Kenora did retain its Manitoba title. With Smith and Westwick in the lineup, Kenora downed the Brandon Wheat Kings 8–6 and 4–1 to sweep the best-of-three series in straight games.

But under the guidelines set here, shouldn't this series be considered just as legitimate a Stanley Cup challenge as the one that followed it?

Apparently the Montreal Wanderers thought so. They announced to the media that they would be in Winnipeg by March 15 and ready to take up the series "with either Brandon or Winnipeg."

In the challenge era of the Stanley Cup, there were only two ways in which a team could win the prized trophy. One was to beat a team in a head-to-head challenge match. And the other was to defeat a team for its own league title.

So, clearly then, the Stanley Cup was definitely on the line in the best-of-three series between Brandon and Kenora—just as it had been when the Wanderers beat the Silver Seven in a league playoff in 1906. And just as it had been when the Silver Seven defeated the Montreal Victorias in the league playoff back in 1903.

The Brandon-Kenora series has never appeared in the Stanley Cup record books, but if justice is rightfully served, it will from now on.

After downing Brandon, the Thistles opened their two-game, total-goal defense of the Cup against Montreal on March 23, 1907. The Wanderers won 7–2 and even though Kenora squeezed to a 6–5 victory in the deciding game, Montreal took the total-goal series 12 goals to 8 and ended Kenora's brief Stanley Cup reign.

Sickness in Seattle: Seattle Slew

The epidemic of Spanish influenza that ended the 1919 Stanley Cup series is believed to have begun at Camp Funston in Kansas during the summer of 1918. The virus was carried overseas to Europe by American soldiers and returned to the shores of North America when the wounded returned in September 1918.

Unlike most flu viruses, which attack the young and the elderly, this one struck hardest at those in the prime of their life. The disease was so lethal that a person could feel fine at breakfast, show symptoms by lunch, and be dead before dinner. First reported in Boston, the flu spread across the continent with alarming speed.

By the middle of October, communities from coast to coast resembled ghost towns. And worst of all, there was no known cure. One of the first athletes to succumb to the disease was Ottawa Senators

Joe Hall

defenseman Hamby Shore. Just 32 years old, the flu claimed his life on October 14, 1918.

Suddenly, when the cool weather of November arrived, the sickness just seemed to stop. Unfortunately, it was a false alarm. The flu would rise again and continue to claim lives across the continent.

That was the scenario in the city of Seattle when the Stanley Cup championship series between Seattle and Montreal was being played in the spring of 1919. It was one of the most exciting, hard-fought, and balanced series ever played. The two clubs battled through five extremely taxing games in nine days, two of which required lengthy overtimes, and still the series was all even at two wins apiece and one tie.

The decisive match was scheduled for the evening of April 1, but when game day arrived, it was determined that many of the Canadiens players were just too ill to participate. Manager George Kennedy, captain Newsy Lalonde, Louis Berlinquette, and Billy Coutu were all confined to bed with high fevers. Two others, Jack McDonald and Joe Hall, were so sick they needed to be hospitalized. To Seattle's credit, they never suggested that the series be forfeited in their favor.

With the weather warming and no relief from the epidemic in sight, hockey officials had no choice but to abandon the series, marking the only time in Stanley Cup history that no winner was declared.

Within a few days, most of the players were feeling well enough to return home. But Joe Hall's condition did not improve and he died in the hospital in Seattle on April 5, 1919. Two years later, George Kennedy also passed away. It was said that he had never fully recovered from his battle with the flu.

The Truth about the Sickness in Seattle

For years, hockey sources have suggested that the Montreal Canadiens picked up the flu virus while visiting Victoria prior to the 1919 Stanley Cup series in Seattle. The truth of the matter is that the Canadiens were never even in Victoria!

The team left Montreal by train on March 10 and played exhibition games in Regina and Calgary on March 13 and 14 before arriving in Vancouver on March 16. Following an exhibition match against the Vancouver Millionaires on March 17, the club took an overnight ferry to Seattle and arrived on the morning of March 18. The Stanley Cup series began the next day.

[l-r] Henri Richard, Jean Beliveau, John Ferguson, and Yvan Cournoyer of the Montreal Canadiens celebrating the series win over the Toronto Maple Leafs, April 13, 1965

THE MECCAS OF HOCKEY

What Does Go on Inside the Locker Room?

In today's multifaceted "on the air—all the time" televised era of sports, focus on the athlete is everywhere, all the time. There are cameras in every imaginable location that a technician and producer can visualize placing them—on the sidelines, on the benches, in the penalty boxes, and in the nets, all showing the athletes and the action from any number of angles.

And though some cameras have been able to show sporadic action and jock-talk from the locker rooms, that prized vestibule remains the sacrosanct domain of the athlete. In the dressing room, the old cliché rings true: "What you see here, what you hear here, when you leave here, it stays here."

Canny Conny's Con Game

S till, some great old yarns seep out of the dressing room from time to time. During the 1942 Stanley Cup finals between Toronto and Detroit, Leafs bench boss Hap Day needed to use a most unusual form of motivation to get his lads back on the beam after falling behind in the series three games to none. He read his troops a letter from an 11-year-old female Leaf fan—who was from Detroit no less. It seems this poor girl was taking some serious ribbing from her

Conn Smythe and Dick Irvin

classmates over the inept play of her "team." Day's sour tone and hound-dog expression struck a nerve with the team and they went out and won the final four games of the series, becoming the only team in professional sports history to win a best-of-seven championship round after losing the first three games.

Canny Conn Smythe also played a key role in that victory. Smythe had already joined the Armed Forces, and control of the team had been delegated to men Smythe clearly felt were his "inferiors." And because he was no longer the "majordomo" around the place, he was regarded as persona nongrata around Maple Leaf Gardens. Until he returned to civilian life, he would be allowed into the building, but by no means would he be allowed into the dressing room.

Smythe knew all this, but he never thought those restrictions would stretch all the way to game seven of the Stanley Cup finals. Yet, when he attempted to enter the players' domain to give a motivational message of his own during the seventh and deciding game of the 1942 finals, he found his way blocked and the premises deemed "off limits."

Well, this was Conn Smythe they were dealing with—the man who raised most of the money he needed to buy the floundering Toronto St. Pats by placing astute bets on underdog teams in Canadian college football games. This was the same man who gathered the capital necessary to buy the rights to King Clancy from the Ottawa Senators by wagering an insane amount of cash on a horse named Rare Jewel in the Gratuity Stakes, one of the richest races of Canadian-bred horseflesh in the country.

Legend tells us that Rare Jewel won that stakes race and Smythe took his bounty, bought Clancy from Ottawa, and watched as the newly adorned Maple Leafs went on to capture their first Stanley Cup only one year later. And we haven't even mentioned his building the facility they were attempting to bar him from.

Besides, most history books fail to mention just how rare Rare Jewel really was. She was a filly with a nose for the bottle and it took a pint of brandy for her to run the race of a lifetime. If Smythe could overcome these odds, how could anyone stop him from entering the Leafs' dressing room with the team down 1–0 in game seven of a series that they had fought so bravely and proudly to come back in?

Well, using might, fright, and cash to do it right, Smythe found his way into the dressing room. He may no longer have been majordomo, but he was still the major. Smythe's well-rehearsed rhetoric reminded his "employees" that they were Canadians, representing their country not only on the ice but also in the hearts and minds of every soldier who was dying on the battlefields of Europe, many of whom were English Canadians and most of whom were Leaf fans.

A tad heavy-handed, to be sure, but it struck a power chord with the boys. It told them that the major still held the reins of power in "this" universe and unless they wanted K rations for breakfast in September, they had better get out there and dispatch the Wings with authority. Sweeney Schriner fired home a pair of markers while Pete Langelle, a journeyman in the right place at the right time, scored the Cup winner as the 1941–42 Maple Leafs team became the comeback kings and a club that is still revered in history.

No Play, No Pay

Another piece of brilliant locker room bargaining came during the Soviet Red Army's first exhibition tour of NHL cities during the 1975–76 season. This time it was Philadelphia Flyers' owner Ed Snider who provided the locker room oration. The Red Army team was a powerhouse unit, featuring many of the same names that had brought the entire country of Canada to the brink of a nervous breakdown during the Series of the Century in 1972. They were undefeated against NHL opponents until they reached Philadelphia's Spectrum, home of the Stanley Cup–winning Flyers, on January 11, 1976.

If the Soviets entered this game feeling a tad queasy, they weren't alone. After all, this was the "Broad Street Bullies" they were facing. It was no secret that numerous "hard-nosed" NHL players often suffered a severe case of the "Philly flu" when it came time to go into the

Philadelphia Flyers versus Soviet Red Army

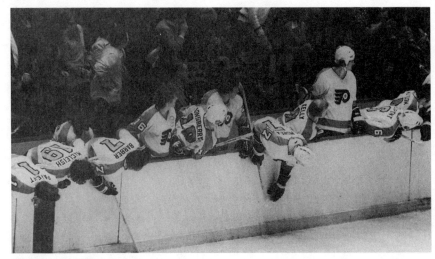

Philadelphia Flyers bench

Spectrum and face the likes of Dave "Hammer" Schultz, "Moose" Dupont, and Bobby "The Clobber" Clarke.

Midway through the first period with the Flyers holding a 1–0 lead, the Soviets took exception to a thundering bodycheck that big Flyer defenseman Ed Van Impe laid on Valery Kharlamov. Without a word of explanation, the team and the coaches left the ice and returned to their locker room.

Snider stormed into the Red Army's locker room and began his rant. Oh, to be a fly on the wall as he read the Reds the riot act. Snider reminded the Soviets that this "goodwill" tour was strictly a "pay-for-play" proposition. If they wanted their cash, they better not dash.

Well, the Russians knew a good-old-fashioned capitalistic threat when they heard one. They returned to the game, more than willing to accept a 4–1 loss on the ice sheet instead of $10,000 loss on the balance sheet.

Take the Trophy and Run

And let's not forget the cool Cup coup Edmonton coach and general manager Glen Sather inflicted on the Philadelphia Flyers prior to game seven of the 1987 Stanley Cup finals. The Flyers were the surprise team of the year, motivated by the maniacal coaching methods of Mike Keenan, driven by the resolute resolve of Rick Tocchet and Tim Kerr, and boosted by the stellar goaltending of freshman Ron Hextall.

It appears that Keenan, knowing the Stanley Cup was in the house and waiting to be presented to the winning club later that evening, wanted to bring the silver chalice into the Philly dressing room to allow his players to bask in its glory. Keenan felt it would be the supreme motivating tool, enough to send this group of overachievers into the Stanley Cup–winner's circle.

The trouble was, he couldn't find the NHL's championship gem. It had disappeared from the security guards assigned to protect it and they were at a loss to explain its whereabouts. Some pundits speculate that "Iron" Mike spent so much time seething at the mystery of the missing mug that his own game plan for game seven may have suffered. As it turns out, Sather, using his in-house network of spies and tattle-tales, learned of the plan and hijacked the Cup before Keenan could get his hands on the trophy. While Keenan cursed, Sather smiled as the Oilers went on to defeat the Flyers 3–1 and win their third Stanley Cup title in four years.

Kevin Lowe and Mark Messier

Guts and Glory

Glen Sather knew more than a little about the rules and regulations of dressing room philosophy and motivation. As a journeyman player with half a dozen pro clubs in both the NHL and WHA, he had learned the hard and fast rules of what it took to survive and succeed in the game of pro hockey. But even he was at a loss to explain how his Edmonton Oilers machine—a well-tuned unit that featured at least six players certain to become members of the Hockey Hall of Fame—could be swept with such efficient ease by the New York Islanders in the 1983 Stanley Cup finals. To a man, the players were confounded by their failure as well. It wasn't until they were leaving the Nassau Coliseum following the Islanders' 4–2 Cup-clinching win in game four that they learned the real secret of success.

As Gretzky, Messier, Coffey, Anderson, Fuhr, and Lowe passed by the Isles' locker room, they saw a sight that shocked and stunned them. Instead of the regaling cheers and champagne-swilling camaraderie that usually follow a Stanley Cup victory, all they heard were moans and groans. Inside the Isles locker room, the battered foot soldiers were nursing their wounds, the stars were getting stitched, and the coaches were still bickering about a missed assignment that had absolutely no effect on the outcome of the game. The Islanders may have been content in their accomplishment, but each of them was painfully aware of the effort and commitment that it took to achieve it. It was a lesson that Gretzky, Messier, and their pals would never forget.

What I Did on My Winter Vacation

For those hockey fans who have wondered what the various NHL coaches did during the great lockout of the 1994–95 season, Winnipeg Jets' bench boss Barry Long put it this way: "I go from locker to locker, pretending the guys are here. You know, give them a little bit of a pep talk. It must be working, because we haven't lost a game yet."

The Rat Patrol

When NHL hockey was just making its first inroads into the state of Florida, the story of Scott Mellanby and the dressing room rat gave the team an instant personality. It also created a rule change that ended one of the game's most enduring traditions.

Early in the Panthers' inaugural campaign in Florida, Mellanby killed a rat that crossed his path in the Florida locker room. Seems he cradled the rodent with the blade of his stick and fired a perfect slapshot off the far wall, high to the stick side, as they say. Monsieur Rat was flattened, and Mellanby became the toast of the town.

From that point on, every time he scored, the Florida faithful would shower the ice surface with plastic rats. "I spent ten years in this league, working hard every night to get my share of goals," the Panthers' captain said, "and now I'm going to go down in history as Rat Man."

When the Panthers finally made it to the Stanley Cup finals in 1996, every time the team scored, the fans would rain rats onto the ice. To the fans, it was a moving tribute to the "little team that could," but to the league and the opposition who had to endure lengthy delays in play while the ice was being scooped clean, it was more than just annoying. Following the season, the NHL introduced new legislation that outlawed showering the ice with rats, bats, or elephants. If the home team's fans insisted on throwing debris, the home team would be penalized.

By definition, the rule also condemned the throwing and tossing of octopus, which had been a part of Detroit Red Wings' postseason ritual for over four decades. There was one caveat to the rule that the league was willing to overlook. If a player scored three goals in a game, fans could still toss their hats onto the ice to celebrate the hat trick. And if the fans had placed their names inside the cap, they could even retrieve them after the match.

Button It

O f course, life inside the locker room can also make even the most mild-mannered players become a little stir-crazy. Take Ray Ferraro, for instance. It's rare when a well-paid, set-for-life player like Ferraro opens his mouth to speak ill of anyone or anything. But that was before he became a member of the Los Angeles Kings. "Our biggest problem is that literally nobody knows each other in this dressing room," Ferraro said after another frustrating night playing before empty seats. "This is the most fragmented dressing room I've seen." Well, suffice to say that Ray wasn't a member of the Los Angeles Kings the following season.

When a House Is Not a Home

O f all the NHL arenas that have come and gone, the New York Islanders' home rink has created the most difficulty for the team, the fans, and the players. Lease troubles and maintenance woes have only added to the difficulties the team is having on the ice. Once, not long ago, when a sewage line backed up and leaked into the Islanders' dressing room, Roger Newton, the Coliseum's general manager, attempted to add some levity to the disaster by saying, "Actually we're trying to get it to flood both locker rooms, just to be fair."

The True Shrine of Hockey

Every sport needs a center stage for its spectacle to be highlighted. Tennis has Wimbledon, baseball has Yankee Stadium, golf has Augusta, soccer has Wembley, and hockey had the Montreal Forum.

There are two million people who feel like they are homeless now. That's what (losing the Forum) feels like to them.

Former Montreal Canadiens defenseman Craig Ludwig after the Forum closed its doors for the last time

The Forum was home to the Montreal Canadiens and the Montreal Maroons, but it was Les Canadiens who made the arena an institution. It seeped history from every doorway and aisle. It reeked tradition from the dressing room to the washroom and it inspired success from the Stanley Cup banners that hung from its rafters to the impressive trophy cases that lined its hallways.

The fans love you here, win or tie.

Steve Shutt

Old Montreal Forum

In the grand old closet that served as the Canadiens' locker room, the faces of the dozens of former members of "*Les Glorieux*" who had been inducted into the Hockey Hall of Fame were grandly displayed on the walls. They seemed to stare down in judgment of the team as they prepared for another night on the ice. And as the players lined up to make the short trek down the hallway toward the ice surface, they were reminded to reflect on the words of inspiration that were written above the doorway—"To you from failing hands we throw the torch; be yours to hold it high."

One Canadiens' veteran remembers one morning during training camp in the late 1960s when a rookie stormed into the dressing room after having been put through the wringer during a tough practice. The

Montreal Forum

freshman tore off his jersey and tossed it into the corner. A hush fell over the room as team captain Jean Beliveau slowly rose from the stool in front of his locker and walked over to pick up the crumbled sweater. Carefully folding it, he brought it back over to the rookie, who was now cowering with fear. Big Jean leaned over and sternly but calmly said; "This is the jersey of the Montreal Canadiens. It must be treated with respect. It never lands on the floor again!" We can assume that the newcomer in question never disrobed in that fashion again.

One-time Canadiens' sniper Stephane Richer also had some poignant memories of the old building. "When we played Saturday night games, the Rocket, Bernie Geoffrion, Jean Beliveau, and Yvan Cournoyer would come to the morning skate and then come into the locker room to shake hands. I'm telling you, it was unbelievable. When we were growing up, all of us, we all wanted to hear Claude Mouton (the Canadiens' long-time public address announcer) say our name at the end of the game, you know, '*Le premier étoile*, the first star.' Even Dano (Ken Daneyko, a teammate of Richer's when both were members of the New Jersey Devils), when we come to the Forum, he goes, '*Le premier étoile*, the third star' . . . which makes no sense, but we all know what he means."

The Loudest Barn in America

Another famous NHL landmark that is no longer with us is the old Chicago Stadium. There has never been and will never be another barn quite like the stadium. From its leather-lunged loonies in the cheap seats, to the majestic swirls of its immense pipe organ, to the heart-pumping renditions of the American national anthem, an evening at the stadium was a night like no other.

Where else would you see lovable louts in the back corner purposely pour beer in the aisle just so they could sit back and roar with delight as they watched some unsuspecting fan slip and slide in the spilled suds?

Where else were the rats treated like royalty? Where else could you find a visitors' dressing room that was so small, even the players had to go outside to change their mind. And then, of course, there was its location. Even Jim Croce's famous song about the south side of

Chicago Stadium

Chicago, "Bad, Bad Leroy Brown," didn't accurately describe just how hostile the neighborhood really was.

Which leads us to Jeremy Roenick's infamous "walk on the wild side."

Shortly after signing his first contract with the Hawks, Roenick decided to walk all the way from the stadium to his hotel room in central Chicago. Now, here's a man who would willingly go toe-to-toe with on-ice bruisers such as Kelly Chase, Donald Brashear, or Tie Domi on the ice. But it took a night on the mean streets of Chicago, strolling all alone with the sirens wailing and the bullets ricocheting, for Roenick to learn what it was like to be truly scared.

When the old barn was demolished and the new facility opened, Roenick went so far as to blame the poor performance of the team on the freshly sanitized new building. "Hey, it's got a nice locker room and everything. Maybe we get too comfortable and bring it out there. In the old place we were chasing cockroaches out of our stalls and we couldn't wait to get out of there."

Maple Leaf Gardens in 1932; photo courtesy City of Toronto Archives

The Carlton Street Cathedral

The one thing I learned was that if you played your heart out, the fans here appreciated it win or lose.

Former Leafs forward Rocky Saganiuk

You don't replace a Maple Leaf Gardens; it's a special place, sacred. We'll never recapture the atmosphere we had in those places. We'll have to create new excitement, new history, I suppose.

Wayne Gretzky

If the Montreal Forum was a shrine, then Maple Leaf Gardens was a cathedral. Actually, it was better known as Pal Hal's Palace or the Carlton Street Cash Box because it was always packed regardless of how badly the Leafs were doing in the standings. And although it didn't hold the same mystique as the Montreal Forum, it still had a special bond with fans across Canada because so many of the early radio and TV broadcasts originated there. One pundit put it this way, "If the two arenas were comedians, the Gardens would be the Three Stooges and the Forum would be Charlie Chaplin. Both popular, successful, revered, and admired, but for entirely different reasons."

"It's always been a shrine for me," said former Oilers and Flames defenseman Steve Smith. "My first game there was an exhibition match in 1981 and I can still remember public address announcer Paul Morris saying, 'Edmonton penalty, Steve Smith, two minutes for cross-checking.' I was so pumped up."

Tiger Williams' most famous quip as a Maple Leaf came after Toronto had taken a one-game lead in a best-of-three series against Pittsburgh in 1978. When asked about the Leafs' chances of ending the series quickly, the Tiger replied, "Them Penguins are done like dinner."

Williams played as though a Maple Leaf was tattooed on his heart during his six seasons with Toronto. He was a combustible performer, tough as nails, and a player who played the modern game with the fury of an "Original Six" role player. "I never wanted to leave the Maple Leafs," Williams said after he appeared on Gardens ice during the closing ceremonies. "It was one of the saddest moments of my life. Last night brought back a lot of those memories."

She's a good old lady. It's going to be sad to see the team move.
Rocky Saganiuk

THE BUS LEAGUES— LIFE IN THE MINORS

Look, You Just Can't Make This Stuff Up!

The old Eastern Amateur Hockey League was a rough and tumble loop that operated up and down the Eastern seaboard of the United States. In order to survive in those days, the league operators needed to provide the fans with something a little more unique than just the game of hockey. So, in the 1930s, the league arranged for Norwegian sweetheart Sonja Henie to become part of the entertainment package. The reigning Olympic figure skater was inked to a professional skating contract, and in between periods she would perform some of her classic moves for the assembled throngs. Not that it all went smoothly. Henie often refused to leave the ice when she was rehearsing, even though the hockey team was scheduled to practice. Well, it took only a couple of well-placed slap shots that zinged off the glass near her head to convince her to share her ice time more prudently.

Grin and Bear It

A nd then there was the skating bear. One of the rituals of spring in New York City is the arrival of the circus, and for decades that meant the New York Rangers would be turfed out of their home for a couple of weeks while the circus held center stage. One of the classic acts that always drew a crowd was the skating bear, a large grizzly that was quite adept at motoring around the big top on roller skates. Tom Lockhart, one of the EHL barons, decided to book the bear to display its talents during the first period intermission of a game between the New York Rovers and the Hershey B'ars.

Well, when the bear showed up, his trainer informed Lockhart he intended to showcase the act on ice, and both he and his grizzled buddy would need ice skates. How Lockhart managed to find said items has escaped through the sands of time, but skates were secured and the act made its way onto the ice. It didn't take long for chaos to roar its ugly head.

Shortly after taking to the ice, the bear broke loose from its leash and went barreling, spinning, slipping, and sliding all around the rink before he was finally restrained and sedated. Needless to say, that act was put on ice.

They Play How Many Periods?

Sometimes the term "nontraditional market" is not strong enough to describe the wide variety of locations where hockey has spread its wings in recent years. The Western Professional Hockey League is one of the newest pro leagues to preach the hockey gospel. The loop features teams in such exotic locales as rural Texas, New Mexico, Arkansas, Louisiana, and Mississippi. And it's not always been a smooth and easy sell.

When the WPHL played its first game on October 16, 1996, a crowd of over 6,000 curious onlookers crammed the Bell County Exposition Center in Belton, Texas, to watch the hometown Central Texas Stampede take on the Waco Wizards.

After the second period horn blew, thousands of fans began to head for the exits. It's not that they were disgusted with the physical contact or unhappy with the performance of the players, it was just that they didn't know hockey had three periods. Everyone figured, like football and basketball, the teams play a pair of halves and then call it a day! After a quick on-site tutorial, most of the fans returned to the rink and watched their team go on to a 5–4 shootout victory.

Hey, I've Got a Great Idea!

ockey's growing popularity in the Deep South has led promoters to try a number of unique and unusual promotions. The Austin Ice Bats of the Western Professional Hockey League once held (and I swear this is true) a "Win Your Own Funeral Night" in which the lucky "winner" was driven off the ice in a hearse after capturing the grand prize—his own casket and a burial plot.

The Lake Charles Ice Pirates held a "Snip and Trip" promotion, sponsored by a local doctor, in which the winner received a vasectomy and a vacation. Chances are if you needed one, you were going to really appreciate the other.

Fans of the Corpus Christi IceRays who mailed their season ticket renewal orders early for the 2000–1 campaign received an invitation to the July 1, 2000, wedding of the team's most popular player, Geoff Bumstead, and his home-grown honey. Not only did the promotion work—more than 1,000 fans actually showed up at the wedding!

So, This Is Why They Call It the Bus League

To say that travel in the Eastern League was an arduous adventure is insulting to the word *arduous.* In the 1960s, the league expanded into numerous nonhockey communities such as Nashville, Knoxville, Greensboro, Jacksonville, and St. Petersburg. There was only one way to get to these towns in those days, and that was riding the road on the bus. Since you sometimes had to travel all day and night, management would rip out a bunch of seats in the back of the bus so the players could plop down a few mattresses and at least pretend to get some shut-eye. "We used to get on a bus in Clinton around 10 on a Sunday night," recalled Pat Kelly, who coached the EHL's Clinton Comets to three straight championships, "and we'd drive for 36 hours to get to Jacksonville to play. We'd go right through, nonstop. They just changed drivers—two men would take turns driving. I sometimes drove the bus myself, just to help them out."

Play at Your Own Risk

Most of the old arenas in the EHL were not built with the safety of the opposing team in mind. The Long Island Ducks played their home games at a facility called Commack Arena. Fans there were known to be a bit rambunctious. To reach their own locker room, players sometimes had to walk under the stands. That meant walking past the concession stands where the beer and the food were sold. Well, where there's beer, there are fans. And where there's fans and beer, there's gonna be fights. Players had to make that trek in tandem, hoping that safety in numbers would ward off the surging spectators.

Even the ice surface wasn't safe. Big John Brophy, an EHL hellion who went on to coach the Toronto Maple Leafs, remembers fans throwing chairs at him. "I'd just moved and needed some new furniture," Broph recalled, "so I grabbed a couple of the nicer ones to take home with me on the bus and threw the rest right back at the fans who had whipped them at me."

Before He Became Baseball Bob

While he was attending the University of Syracuse in New York State, esteemed baseball analyst Bob Costas honed his journalistic chops on the hockey beat as a play-by-play man for the Syracuse Blazers of the old North American Hockey League. Early on, this created a couple of unique problems for the greenhorn reporter.

First of all, he knew nothing about the game. To prepare himself for his first night on the job "I went to all of the games I could to learn as much as I could." Costas recalls, "and on the day of the game I sat down and talked with anyone that knew about hockey, and I studied and restudied everything I had. But on the night of the game, the other team decided to get brand-new uniforms with all new numbers on them."

And if that wasn't bad enough, on the bus trip home Costas made a quip that upset the Blazers' enforcer, bully, and goon, Billy Goldthorpe, whom the character Oggie Ogilthorpe in the classic hockey movie *Slap Shot* is based on. Goldthorpe was actually ready to toss Costas off the bus—while the bus was still moving, by the way—before a few of the veteran Blazers were able to put out the flames in Goldthorpe's fiery temper and save Costas's bacon. Otherwise, one of the most passionate voices dedicated to saving the game of baseball might never have had an opportunity to be so eloquent.

Jim McGeough; photo courtesy City of Toronto Archives

Put Me In, Coach

The minor leagues may be minor in size and stature, but they still have major league rules. Former NHL sniper Jim McGeough found this out the hard way. At the time, McGeough was playing with the Dallas Freeze in the CHL. Even in the bus leagues, curfews are necessary and enforced. One evening, McGeough decided to test the waters and see if those hard and fast rules applied to former NHL stars. McGeough tripped the night fantastic and didn't return to his hotel until the early hours of the morning, sure that no one was the wiser.

However, there are grapevines everywhere, even in the bus leagues. The coach learned of his player's late-night ways and decided to prove to Mr. McGeough that he wasn't blind. So, he nailed McGeough to the bench. Still, McGeough didn't clue into why he was spending so much time on the pine. Finally, with only minutes to go in the game, Jimmy decided to undo his skates, since it didn't appear he was going to see the ice that night. But with less than a minute to go, the coach gave McGeough the shoulder tap to hit the ice and our hero, eager to please, catapulted over the boards. The only problem was his loosened skates stayed on the bench. So, there he was, on the ice in his sock feet with the whole bench rolling in the aisles. Quickly and quietly, he hopped back on the bench. They tell me he plays in Wichita now.

Stay on the Bus

The one rule that changed the face of hockey forever wasn't even introduced to the game until the mid-1960s. Before that time, teams carried only one goaltender. But with the introduction of curved blades and increased television exposure, fans and sponsors were getting tired of waiting for the one and only twine tender to get sewn up and tossed back into the fray after taking an errant puck in the head. So, the league introduced new legislation that required all teams to have a second goaltender dressed and ready for action sitting on the bench. Soon every loop around the country adopted the new rule. That has resulted in some unique moments. Philadelphia Flyers trainer Dave Settlemyre had to suit up a couple of times when one of the Flyers' goalies couldn't dress and a backup couldn't be found in time. But at least he could skate.

That's not always the case. In the lower leagues, teams can't afford the luxury of having their trainer suit up as the spare goalie. In 1998, the Fort Worth Fire of the CHL discovered they were without a backup netminder and they were adamant that they weren't going to forfeit the game. The team's bus driver, a brave soul to say the least, suggested he be given the job. After all, he wasn't going anywhere without the rest of the team, and he would never be called upon to play. So, he was recruited, dressed, and sent to the bench. There's only one thing he forgot to tell the team. He couldn't skate. And there was only one thing they forgot to tell him. To get to the bench, you had to skate all the way across the ice. So, as he skittered, slid, and spun his way over to the bench, the crowd went into hysterics, yelling, "Bus driver, bus driver." Although the man behind the wheel later took it all in with a smile, he never volunteered to get off the bus again.

Disrobing from the Rafters

When the Cincinnati Cyclones retired Paul Lawless's jersey, many of his former teammates felt that the only way to truly commemorate his career in Cincinnati would be to hang a robe from the rafters, not a sweater. Lawless may have flourished during his career with the Cyclones, collecting 132 goals and 305 points in 255 games, but it was the robe that made him unique.

That's right. Lawless wore a robe. He broke the time-honored code of "letting it all hang out" in the dressing room by donning a robe while strolling through the locker room area. No one had ever seen that before. Chris Cichocki, who was Lawless's teammate with Cincinnati from 1993–96, said the thought of Lawless sitting there, wearing that %^%$% robe, still makes him chuckle. Todd Hawkins, who played with Lawless in Milwaukee, also laughs about the robe. "Lawly's the only guy who was able to wear the robe and get away with it because it was funny, and so was Lawly," said Hawkins.

Adds Cichocki: "When I roomed with Lawless the last couple of years, I roomed with his cigars. That's what cut my career short, I was breathing in that cigar smoke."

Tom Martin

JUNIOR LEAGUES, SENIOR STORIES

Do You Get Tires with that Bus?

Believe it or not, former NHL forward and university star Tom Martin was traded for a bus. And it gets better than that! It was a used bus. At the time, Martin was playing for the University of Denver Pioneers, but he had mentioned he would leave school and play major junior if he could play in his hometown of Victoria. His WHL rights were held by Seattle, which was more than willing to swap them to Victoria if the proper deal could be arranged. The clubs met to discuss various combinations of prospects and players, but both sides were having difficulty finding a match. Until someone mentioned the bus.

The vehicle in question had been purchased by the Spokane Flyers in 1981 for $60,000. When the Flyers franchise folded, the Victoria Cougars bought the bus for a song, but they were unwilling to pay the exorbitant customs, excise, and sales taxes necessary to get the beast across the border. So, when the Breakers suggested they would be willing to swap the rights to Martin for the bus, it sealed the deal.

"Actually, it was just the down payment on the bus, about $35,000," Breakers' owner John Hamilton remembered, "still, it might have been the best deal I ever made." The official record of the transaction reads as follows: "The WHL's Seattle Breakers traded the rights of leftwinger Tom Martin to the Victoria Cougars for a used bus."

And the tires, presumably.

Lost in the Translation

If a guy's in the room, yelling or bitching, I've got no idea what he's saying . . . I don't read Russian, so I don't know if the papers are saying good things or bad.

Goaltender Vincent Riendeau, one of the few North America–born ex-NHLers to sign and play in Russia

Vincent Riendeau, shown here with St. Louis, played in Russia with Lada Togliatti in 1998–99 and 1999–2000.

They Traded How Many Players and for Whom?

Unlike the OHL and the QMJHL, which hold a draft of the top 16-year-olds each year, the Western Hockey League holds a bantam draft to select the top 15-year-old prospects in the region. The 1982 WHL bantam draft was one of the wildest in league history. Just prior to the selection process's getting under way, the Regina Pats acquired Rick Herbert, a 15-year-old rearguard who was one of the most-sought-after bantam-aged players in WHL history. He must have been, because five other teams wanted him and it cost the Pats seven players to get him. In a complicated multiteam agreement, Regina traded Byron Lomow, Tim Brown, and Kevin Pylypow to Kamloops for the draft's third pick. Darryl Watts, Scott Wilson, Peter Hayden, and Scott Gerla were given to Kelowna for the Wings' agreement not to select Herbert with the first pick of the bantam draft. The Pats selected Herbert, and he went on to play five years in the WHL, also suiting up with Spokane, Brandon, and Portland—three of the teams that were striving to sign him in the first place. He did appear in three games with Saginaw of the IHL at the end of his junior career, but he never played professionally again.

Glen Goodall

Young and Restless

Another remarkable selection occurred in the 1982 WHL bantam draft. Seattle choose a 12-year-old from Thompson, Manitoba, named Glen Goodall, and he became the youngest player to ever be selected in the WHL draft. And that record is safe, because new rules were introduced to prevent clubs from selecting players who are still of atom age. The Breakers had to wait two years before the kid could even suit up and play, but it was worth the wait.

Goodall was just 14 when he played his first game with the Seattle Breakers on October 10, 1984. It was a 12–3 loss in Regina. "My parents were here tonight," he said at the time, "and they'll follow us around on the rest of our eastern swing, and they might take a trip out to Seattle and I'll see them at Christmas, so it won't be too bad." As for his first game, he said: "I thought I played okay in the third period. When you're down by a lot of goals, it's hard to keep it up." He would go on to play his entire junior career with Seattle, collecting 573 points to become the club's all-time leading points leader and the second leading scorer in WHL history. His size kept him out of the NHL, but he fashioned a terrific career for himself in Europe.

Roydon Gunn

Keep Your Head in the Game

Roydon Gunn, a goalie with the CHL's Memphis RiverKings, devised a unique way to propose to his girlfriend. As the official "voice" of the Kings, his girlfriend would skate out onto the ice before each game and sing the National Anthem. On this particular night, she did her routine, but as she turned to leave, Gunn was right beside her. He dropped to his knees (his coach, who could become exasperated at Gunn's sprawling style, was heard to say, "Well, he's had lots of practice doing that") and he proposed to her, right there on the spot. The crowd went nuts, twice. First, when she accepted his proposal and second when the nervous suitor allowed the first four shots he faced to get by him. Gunn was yanked from the net and spent the rest of the evening watching, and wishing, from the bench.

Cy Denneny

STRANGER THAN FICTION

Ding, Dong, Dell, Denneny's in the Well

On February 20, 1924, the first-place Ottawa Senators and the second-place Montreal Canadiens were scheduled to meet in a key NHL tilt at the Mount Royal Rink in Montreal. Despite a heavy snowfall, a large crowd had filled the arena in time for the 8:30 start but the Senators never showed up. At shortly after 10, it was announced that the game had been postponed and would be rescheduled for the following evening. As the denizens were departing the arena, many had the same question on their minds: what happened to the Senators?

Earlier that day, the Senators had departed the nation's capital on the noon train. Now, normally, the 90-mile trek to Montreal would have taken no more than two hours, leaving plenty of time for the club to have a quick pregame skate, a nap, a meal and still be at the rink ready for their showdown with the Habs. However, by 5 that afternoon, the train had barely reached Hawkesbury, which was only the halfway point of the journey. The train crept along at a snail's pace for a few more miles before becoming completely snowbound at a tiny outpost called Cushing Junction.

Since this was supposed to be a quick and uneventful trip, there were few items of food on board. Ottawa teammates King Clancy and Cy Denneny set out on foot to rustle up some provisions. Some reports say they were trying to find food, others say they were in search of milk for a baby who was on board. The reason they left soon became moot, anyway. There was something more serious that needed to be taken care of. During their search, Denneny tripped and fell down a well-concealed well. Miraculously, he was unhurt. The only explanation that could be given for his lack of injury was that he was protected and cushioned by the thick blanket of snow that had accumulated at the bottom of the well's shaft. After all, it was the biggest blizzard to hit the area in over two decades. Somehow, through the darkness and the snow, his teammates were able to pry Denneny out of the well, but that didn't help the Senators' cause all that much.

As it turned out, the entire team and the rest of the passengers were stranded on the train all night. They finally arrived in Montreal at 8:30 the next morning—without food, sleep, and almost without Denneny. Needless to say, the Senators were not firing on all cylinders later that evening, losing to the Habs 3–0.

The Rangers Jinx

It is said that the New York Rangers' Stanley Cup jinx, a 54-year-long ride of ineptitude that stretched from 1940 until 1994, actually began when the Rangers' brass burned the mortgage to Madison Square Garden in the bowl of the Stanley Cup following the team's victory in 1940.

The Curse of Muldoon

O ne of the enduring myths that has filtered down through the ice shavings of time has been the Muldoon Curse. It seems that when Pete Muldoon was fired as Chicago Blackhawks coach after the 1926–27 season, he vowed he would avenge what he considered to be an unfair dismissal. After all, he led the team into the playoffs in their inaugural season but management still decided to go in another direction. Well, Muldoon decreed that the only direction the Hawks were going to go was down. It was written that he placed a curse on the team that guaranteed the club would never finish in first place.

For decades, it appeared that Muldoon's conjuring of black magic was working. The Blackhawks went over 40 years without finishing at the top of the standings until they finally broke the spell with a first-place finish in the 1966–67 season. Even then, true believers of the Muldoon Moan pointed out that winning the NHL regular season crown in 1966–67 made losing to a third-place bunch of geriatric old-timers like the Toronto Maple Leafs even more painful. It wasn't until some time later that it was disclosed that the curse was nothing more than a phony folly dreamed up by a sportswriter in 1941 to sell a few newspapers.

And where was Muldoon during all of this? Why didn't he step forward to deny his mystical powers? Well, Muldoon may not have placed the curse, but in some ways, he seemed to be cursed himself. He died in March 1929, only two years after losing his one and only NHL coaching job.

Hockey's First Labor Dispute

We've all heard the whining before. The owners cry poor. The players only want what is fair. The owners need a salary cap. The players won't accept one. It looks like a winter without hockey. No, this isn't 1994 or even 2002. This was 1911 and the professional game of hockey was facing its first labor dispute.

The 1909–10 season had seen great upheaval in the game. By offering huge salaries, the new National Hockey Association had won its war with the rival Canadian Hockey Association, but the battle exacted a price of financial pain. The owners looked to recoup some of their financial losses in 1910–11 by imposing a salary cap of $5,000 per team. Bruce Stuart, captain of the Ottawa Senators, stressed that the players would never accept any kind of salary "cap" and he threatened to organize his own league. Art Ross was also involved in organizing this new "players'" league, but the owners did not take the threat seriously until the players stopped agreeing to contracts. "We are all suffering from writer's cramp," quipped Stuart, "and we cannot sign up."

But the players' revolt was short-lived. Stuart was unable to get arena owners to support his new league. They reasoned that the NHA offered guaranteed purses while Stuart's new league offered only headaches. Soon, the idea of a new league was abandoned and the players began signing contracts with their old teams. The dispute had lasted about a month and though no regular-season games were lost, training camps had been disrupted.

While there is evidence that many owners either ignored the salary cap or found ways around it, Bruce Stuart never benefited from his actions. After having to accept a $650 offer from Ottawa, Stuart retired after playing only four games. Art Ross continued to fight for players' rights and almost got barred from hockey for his trouble. Ironically,

Ross would go on to have a long career in management with the NHL's Boston Bruins and, when push came to profit, he would have to adopt the very stance he fought so hard against when he was a player.

The Silver Screen

The most famous—and the most popular—movie about the sport of hockey that has ever been produced is *Slap Shot*, a tale about a fourth-rate hockey team in a third-rate league. The flick could have easily disappeared from the lexicon of cinematic and hockey history if it wasn't for the names of the talent that put the movie together and the brilliance of its execution. Directed by George Roy Hill, who already had blockbuster hits like *Butch Cassidy and the Sundance Kid* and *The Sting* on his résumé, it starred Paul Newman, who was still a matinee idol in those days. It featured an array of rough and tumble characters who looked, sounded, and acted like real hockey players. That's because many of the characters were based on real players who had spent their lives toiling in leagues so far beneath the NHL that they never even bothered to dream about making it to the show anymore.

Based on a script written by Nancy Dowd, the movie borrowed from the antics of the old Eastern Hockey League and the North American Hockey League. Dowd's husband, Ned, who played the immortal Oggie Ogilthorpe in the movie, did the majority of the research for the script.

But this painstaking in-depth examination of low-rung hockey wasn't done in the press box or in the library. No, Ned did his hard-core research on the ice, as a member of the Johnstown Jets and the Kalamazoo Wings. Ned was a star at Bowdoin College, an NCAA Division II powerhouse, before spending a couple of seasons riding the bus in the minors.

It was while he was at Bowdoin that Ned met Michael Ontkean, who was a top scoring forward with the University of New Hampshire. By the time *Slap Shot* was ready to begin production, Ontkean had traded his skates for scripts and was a fairly well-known TV actor, having appeared in "The Partridge Family" and "Longstreet." He was a natural to play the talented but cynical college graduate Ned Braden. His wife in the film was played by Lindsay Crouse, who later married playwright David Mamet and appeared in some of his films when he turned his attention from the stage to the screen.

Reggie Dunlop and Ned Braden

Although the project had star quality names "above the title," it was the lesser lights who stole the show and gave the film its character, comedy, and charisma. The Hanson Brothers (David Hanson, Steve and Jeff Carlson) were all professional hockey players who lit up the screen with every appearance. Yvon Barrette shone as the asthmatic goaltender Denis Lemieux, and character actor Strother Martin hit all the right notes as the owner looking for a way out of hockey and a way out of town. Swoosie Kurtz (*Liar, Liar*), M. Emmett Walsh (*Blood Simple* and 80 other movies to his credit), Melinda Dillon (*Close Encounters*), and Jerry Houser (*Summer of '42*) all added charm and well-honed performances to what could have been nothing more than a no-brainer, foul-mouthed and violent tale about hockey. Thanks to a script with a lady's touch and performances by thoughtful actors who realized they had something special cooking, we received a delightful, honest, and frank look at the violence, characters, and politics of hockey.

The Chiefs on the bench

But what most people remember is the comedy, so here are some key lines from the movie.

This young man has had a very trying rookie season, what with the litigation, the notoriety, his subsequent deportation to Canada, and that country's refusal to accept him, well, I guess that's more than most 21-year-olds could handle.

The radio introduction of Oggie Ogilthorpe

Are you crazy? Those guys are retards!

Reggie Dunlop

I got a good deal on those boys. The scout said they showed a lot of promise.

Joe McGrath

They brought their $%^&^% toys with 'em!

Reggie Dunlop

I'd rather have 'em playing with their toys than playing with themselves.

Joe McGrath

They're too dumb to play with themselves!

Reggie Dunlop

Icing happen when the puck go down, bang, before the other guy, nobody dere, you know, my arm go up, the game stop then start back up.

Goaltender Denis Lemieux describes icing

You go to the box, you know, two minute by yourself, you feel shame, you know, and then you get free.

Goaltender Denis Lemieux on taking a penalty

Donaldson, I'm telling ya, he jumped us. Gloves off, stick down, no warning, he challenged the Chiefs! Called us names. But Dave was there.

Reggie Dunlop

Dave's a killer.

Hanson Brother

Yeah, Dave's a killer, a killer!

Team

Dave's a mess.

Trainer

Get out on the ice—let 'em know you're there. Get that stick in his side—let 'em know you're there! Put a little lumber in his teeth—let 'em know you're there!

Reggie Dunlop

Bleed all over 'em, let 'em know you're there.

Ned Braden

I want to win that championship tonight, but I want to win it clean. Old-time hockey. Eddie Shore, Toe Blake, Dit Clapper— those guys were the greats!

Reggie Dunlop

After his rookie season, Bobby Orr won the Norris Trophy as the NHL's top defenseman eight consecutive times beginning in 1967–68.

Number Four, Bobby Orr

I've been gifted. The world is full of people who not only haven't been gifted, but have had some things taken away from them. All I have to do is see one of them, some little girl who can't walk, and then I don't think I'm such a hero anymore.

Bobby Orr

If Howie Morenz revolutionized the game of hockey in the 1920s, then Bobby Orr redefined the sport forever. No player, with the exception of Wayne Gretzky, has dominated, controlled, and restructured a sport like Robert Gordon Orr. And as great as the Great One was, some shinny scholars still argue that even his incredible style, vision, and talent pale in comparison to the attributes that Bobby Orr brought to the arena every time he laced up his skates. Well, that is not a debate for us to adjudicate. Let us just say this: there will never be another Wayne Gretzky just as surely as there will never be another Bobby Orr.

The best thing about being hired as coach of the Boston Bruins was that I was coach of the team for which Bobby Orr was a player. Mind you I didn't say that I'd coached Bobby Orr because that would be the most presumptuous thing any coach could ever say. He was the greatest hockey player I have ever seen, Gordie Howe and Wayne Gretzky included. The greatest hockey player who ever lived, Bobby Orr, and I love him.

Don Cherry

There's no doubt that somebody, some day, would have finally tapped the rich vein of Orr that was lying unfound and unsigned in the town of Parry Sound, Ontario. Well, it was the great fortune of the

Boston Bruins to be the first prospectors to mine the site. It's not that the Bruins were given a hot tip or had privileged information, it was more a matter of dumb luck and blind faith.

If a player comes along who is better then Bobby Orr, may the Good Lord let me be alive to see him, because he is going to be one hell of a player to watch.

Milt Schmidt

Before the Amateur Draft was introduced, NHL organizations could sponsor as many teams across the country as they wanted to. By sponsoring a team, the NHL club would provide some funding for uniforms and arena maintenance. They would also hold the rights to any players who were with those teams. When the Boston Bruins first discovered Bobby Orr, the team he was performing with in Parry Sound was not sponsored by any NHL franchise, which meant the rights to Orr and every other hockey playing tyke in the region were up for grabs. That would soon change.

Kid, I don't know what you're getting paid, but it isn't enough.

Ted Green to Bobby Orr after one of his first practices in 1966

Young Bobby Orr began his love affair with hockey when he was only two years old. A friend of Bobby's dad bought the future Hall-of-Famer his first pair of skates but they were too big for the wee lad. Doug Orr stuffed the toes of the skates with paper, slipped them onto the feet of his young son, and sent him off to play with the big boys. Imagine his surprise when he saw that his son seemed to be a natural. Before long, Bobby started playing shinny with all the boys in the neighborhood. He learned a lot about dodging, passing, and controlling the puck in those games. While he was still in kindergarten, young Bobby was already playing in the Squirt Hockey League.

By the time he was nine years of age, he had already won an MVP award in the Pee-Wee Division. He was smaller than the other guys, but he had heart, courage, and stamina. Bobby continually drilled himself on improving his skills, spending countless hours on developing his speed, stick handling, and turning both ways with equal dexterity. It was during these sessions that he began to develop the fast spin for which he became famous.

As the #1 attraction in the game today, young Mr. Orr figures to cause a wave of insomnia among rival coaches. How do they prevent him from making their antelope look like water-buffalo with a touch of hepatitis?

Famed sportswriter Milt Dunnell

By 1960, Bobby Orr was already somewhat of a legend in the Parry Sound area, but his star had not yet risen in the east. Later that year, the Parry Sound Bantam All-Stars were playing in a tournament and there wasn't exactly a rich assortment of NHL scouts on hand. But one who was in attendance was Wren Blair, an eagle-eyed expert on spotting hockey talent. Blair was at the tournament to scout two other boys, but he couldn't keep his eyes off the kid wearing jersey #2, who skated circles around the other lads, had a keen eye, and wasn't afraid to muck it up in the corners with teenagers twice his size. Blair was convinced he had just seen the future of hockey and its name was Bobby Orr.

Why did Larry Bird look up at the Boston Garden Ceiling during the playing of the National Anthem? No one knew until a night in 1988 when he explained that he was looking at Bobby Orr's #4.

Bob Ryan, *Boston Globe*

After some tough negotiating, Blair got Bobby's and his father Doug's names on a contract. All Blair had to do was sponsor every team in the Parry Sound region and tell the Orrs that the Bruins were going to put a major junior team in Oshawa so that Bobby could play closer to home. Bobby Orr went on to play five seasons with Oshawa, taking the club to the Memorial Cup finals in 1966 with 36 points in only 12 games. By the time training camp rolled around to start the 1966–67 NHL season, Orr was in a Bruins uniform and the game of hockey would never be quite the same.

I know what he does to a team because I experienced it when we played together in the Canada Cup. We were like a bunch of kids on a pond waiting for someone to come along and organize us. When he walked in the room, we knew we would be all right.

Hall-of-Fame defenseman Denis Potvin

I'd give him my knees if it would help him play again.

Longtime teammate Don Awrey

We hated to check him. We respect him so much that we don't want to do anything to damage those knees.

Former Atlanta Flames defenseman Richard Mulhern

He was such a package of grace and elegance that you would get caught watching him, then the horror would set in about what he was about to do to you.

Bill Clement, hockey analyst

I might as well enjoy it [Norris Trophy] now, because I expect it's going to belong to Bobby Orr from now on.

Harry Howell, Norris Trophy recipient in 1966–67

You can say about each of the great players: He's a good skater, or a good stick-handler, or he has a great shot, but something is always missing. Bobby Orr has it all. He is the best I've seen—ever!

Jacques Plante

I believe Doug Harvey was the best all-round defenseman I've ever seen. Simply put, however, Bobby Orr had the greatest impact of any player to come along in my lifetime. He earned his place in hockey history by single-handedly changing the game from the style played in my day to the one we see today. In my mind there can be no greater legacy.

Jean Beliveau

He was so dominant. Bobby was the greatest defenseman who ever played the game as far as I'm concerned. I believe in my heart that he changed the face of the game.

Phil Esposito

Overall I can fairly safely say Bobby Orr impressed me more than anybody with his tremendous talents. In Bobby's first NHL game he laid the lumber to my head. Later I gave him a pretty good shot with my elbow, just to let the kid know I wasn't washed up yet.

Gordie Howe

Bobby Orr

What's in a Number?

I don't think you ever stopped Bobby Orr. You contained him.
He was too talented and too great a player. When we played the
Bruins and Bobby had to give up the puck it was a good play.

Larry Robinson

O ne of the most famous photographs in hockey history features
the image of Bobby Orr soaring through the air with his arms
spread wide and his face in a state of permanent delirium—
moments after scoring the overtime goal that brought the Stanley Cup
title to the Boston Bruins.

Bobby would drive to the net injured, he would drive to the net
hurt. He played that way every night.

Derek Sanderson

The goal in question was scored on May 5, 1970, against the St.
Louis Blues. The puck was poked past Blues goaltender Glenn Hall by
Bobby Orr, who was wearing jersey #4, of course. It was his fourth goal
of the postseason, scored during the fourth period (albeit overtime) of
the fourth game of the 1970 Stanley Cup finals. The man who tripped
him and sent him flying into history was Noel Picard, who was also
wearing #4.

The Golden Jet

Always keep your composure. You can't score from the penalty box; and to win, you have to score.

Bobby Hull

I wouldn't urinate in his ear if his brain was on fire!
Bobby Hull, discussing a Montreal Canadiens forward he didn't particularly like

One of the greatest attributes of Bobby Hull was his undeniable love for his fans. Few players, even then, would stop during the pregame skate to sign autographs, but Bobby Hull always did. He learned early on how special a kind word or gesture from an athlete can be to an impressionable youngster. When Hull's parents took him by train from Belleville to Toronto to see his first NHL game, he was only 10 years old. The Maple Leafs were playing the Detroit Red Wings, and their rivalry was one of the greatest in all of sports. That night at Maple Leaf Gardens, the future Golden Jet got both Gordie Howe's and Ted Lindsay's autographs. Bobby Hull was especially inspired by the way the two Detroit superstars treated the fans. Bobby followed their example and he was always there to sign autographs for his fans.

When Bobby Hull started up the ice with that puck . . . Buddy, he'd lift you out of your chair every time. Didn't matter if he scored or not.

Chicago Blackhawks fan

Nothing much has changed. After the All-Star Game in Montreal in 1993, I watched Hull take 15 minutes to sign an autograph while we

Ulf Nilsson, Bobby Hull, and Anders Hedberg lit up the World Hockey Association with the Winnipeg Jets beginning in 1973–74.

were traveling to one of the special galas being held to commemorate the event. He only put pen to paper—or in this case marker to Styrofoam target—when the bus was stopped at a red light, so his signature would be legible and the mark of the champion would be precise.

Without those two kids [Anders Hedberg and Ulf Nilsson], I probably would've retired three years ago.

Bobby Hull

Hull's assault on the NHL record book was derailed when he took the money and ran to the WHA, but he never wanted to leave Chicago. When the WHA officials approached him, he half-jokingly said, "Give me a million bucks and I'll join the league," never believing for a second they could ever muster up that kind of cabbage. But when they did, he refused to back down from the promise he made to them. That league lasted seven years, and many still believe it was because Bobby Hull kept his word.

After the demise of the WHA, Hull returned to the NHL with the Winnipeg Jets. In February 1980, he was traded to the Hartford Whalers, where he shared his final skate through the NHL spotlight with the only man who could ever outshine him, Gordie Howe. Actually, it wasn't the end of the Golden Jet's brilliant career. Prior to the 1981–82 season, the New York Rangers went to Sweden to play in a four-team tournament known as the Dagen Nyheter Cup. Hull went over with the club in one last-ditch effort to see if he had one more season of hockey left in his legs. He performed admirably in Sweden, collecting a goal and an assist in four games. But while the spirit was willing, the bones and the body were not, so he hung 'em up for the last time.

I thought it was one of the greatest moments of my life. I had 23 years of professional hockey and loved every moment. Like Yogi Berra said, "It's déjà vu all over again." Brett Hull has one more than his dad. He's done a masterful job.

Bobby Hull after son Brett surpassed him on the NHL's all-time scoring list

Mr. Hockey Lambastes Leapin' Louie

O
ne of the most infamous incidents in hockey history occurred the evening New York Rangers defenseman "Leaping" Louie Fontinato decided to test the mettle of Gordie Howe. The Rangers had been touting Fontinato as the toughest player in hockey. A New York–based magazine called *Look* even did a six-page picture spread on him, showing him flexing his muscles and looking mean. Whenever the Rangers played the Wings, Fontinato made sure he was on the ice with Howe, jabbing at him, jowling at him, and generally causing all kinds of on-ice havoc. "The idea was to distract me," Howe recalled. Well, after a few altercations with the Rangers' goon, Mr. Hockey decided that enough was enough. There was only one way to

Gordie Howe, at left, Sid Abel, and "Terrible" Ted Lindsay formed the potent Production Line for the Red Wings in 1947–48.

make this creep go away and that was to teach him a lesson he would never forget.

It happened at Madison Square Garden in front of a full house of Manhattan maniacs. "Red Kelly and Eddie Shack were in a fight behind our net, and I'm leaning on the net, watching it," Howe remembered; "then I recalled a bit of advice I'd received from Ted Lindsay: Always be aware of who's out on the ice with you. I took a peek and sure enough, there was Louie with his gloves off and coming my way. I truly thought he was going to sucker-punch me. If he had, it would have been all over for me. I pretended I didn't see him, and when he swung, I just pulled my head aside and that honker of his was right there, and I drilled it. That first punch was what did it. It broke his nose a little bit."

Broke his nose a little bit. A little bit? With that one punch, Howe made mincemeat of Fontinato's face, shoving his proboscis halfway around his head, blackening his eyes and turning the ice surface of the Garden into a pool of crimson tide. It certainly solidified Howe's well-deserved reputation as the NHL's toughest player. Even Howe's greatest rival on the ice, the immortal Rocket Richard, admitted, "I have never seen a greater hockey player, I mean a more complete player. Gordie Howe does everything and does it well." Chicago star Bobby Hull was just as succinct—"I wish I was half the player Gordie was," he said. And he meant it.

Clear the Track

One of the most colorful characters to ever grace the ice surfaces of the NHL was Eddie "Clear the Track, Here Comes" Shack, a whirling dervish of energy, emotion, and inertia. Shack could play it anyway you wanted it. He could be tough and slug it out with any and all comers. He could be a pesky checker who would be over his opponent like a bad rash. And he could pop the pill when his team needed an offensive surge. Shack scored at least 20 goals a season for five different teams, but he is best remembered for his days with the Toronto Maple Leafs.

One memorable Saturday night on national TV, the Leafs were being pummeled and humbled by the lowly Boston Bruins to the tune of 11–0. Shack hadn't seen the ice since the first period, and the remaining fans, anxious for anything to keep their attention and fight off the boredom started chanting, "We want Shack!" Finally, coach Punch Imlach relented and gave Shack the shoulder tap with the simple instruction to just "Get on the damn ice." Shack leaped over the boards and raced around the ice, much to the delight of the die-hard throng. Just as the referee was about to drop the puck to commence play, Shack roared over to the Leafs' bench, where he was met by the rocket-red glare of a not-too-amused Coach Imlach. "Hey, Punch," Eddie said, "I forgot to ask, did you want me to tie it or win it?"

Another example of the Shack attack came when he was with the Boston Bruins. One night both he and Derek Sanderson were getting stitched up in the trainer's room after a rather entertaining set-to. Shack went in after Sanderson, and Turk told the trainer to stitch up the veteran first. Eddie refused the offer, saying, "Stitch the kid up, I'll wait. He's the only guy on the team that passes to me."

Once while he was still shuffling through the minors, Shack had a brutal stick fight with Larry Zeidel, one of the toughest guys to ever take to the ice in the era of "old-time hockey." Both players were tossed out of the game and sent to the showers. After they had cooled their heels in the dressing room, they both sat in the stands to watch the remainder of the game. Zeidel spied Shack sitting in the front row and ran over and started laying haymakers on the side of Eddie's head. Afterward, Zeidel rationalized his actions by saying, "Shack's going up to the NHL any day now, and I'm staying here in the AHL. I just figured I wouldn't get another shot at him."

If only that were true. Late in the 1967–68 season, Shack was playing for the Boston Bruins and Zeidel was back in the NHL for the first time in 14 years, patrolling the blueline with the expansion Philadelphia Flyers. The roof of the Philadelphia Spectrum had just collapsed because of a heavy snowfall, and the team was forced to play the remainder of their "home" games on the road, mostly in Quebec City, where their farm team was located. But on this particular evening— March 7, 1968—the Flyers and the Bruins were playing at Maple Leaf Gardens in Toronto. Midway through the match, Zeidel and Shack met up again, and the result was even uglier than the first time they had crossed paths nearly a decade earlier. Zeidel and Shack engaged in a horrific stick duel that left both men cut and bleeding and gave the game another black eye. It was one of the very few black marks to scar the otherwise clean résumé of Edward Philip Shack.

The Elixir of Hockey

Toronto Maple Leafs coach Pat Quinn once observed that there were no magic wands you could just wave to turn a loser into a winner overnight. Well, if that's true someone forgot to tell the New York Rangers during the 1950–51 season.

The 1950–51 campaign was a tough one for the Broadway Blueshirts. Just months after coming within a whisker of winning the Stanley Cup, the Broadway Blues were floating under the .500 mark and were in real danger of missing the playoffs. And every Rangers fan knew that if you could get a ticket to the dance, you could still be waltzing late into the postseason night, just like the Rangers did when they surprised the hockey universe in 1950. Some strange magic was going to be needed if this edition of the Blues was going to equal the heroics of the previous year's team.

It took a local restaurant owner named Gene Leone and a clever sports writer named Jim Burchard to come up with the formula to save the Blueshirts. Leone was a huge Rangers fan, but he and Burchard must have been sipping a little more than coffee when they hatched their birdbrained scheme. Leone decided to create a wonder drink that would pull the Rangers out of the doldrums and propel them toward the Stanley Cup playoffs. And hey, he figured, it would provide a public relations boost for his fledgling bar and even boost the spirits of Broadway's favorite ice-time boys.

Leone went to work mixing, fixing, spilling, combining, and distilling a mixture of delicious fruit juices and an ounce or two of vintage wine to produce an "elixir" that would cure the Rangers' blues. Over the Christmas holidays, he and his now (probably, but who knows for sure) soused newspaper crony "perfected" their concoction, poured it into a huge black bottle, and presented it to the players as the "cure to end

Frankie Eddolls, shown here in a Blackhawks jacket, was one of several Rangers who seemed to become a better player after drinking Leone's Magic Elixir in 1950–51.

all ills." Well, Leone and Burchard must have had the buttery tongues and slippery dialect of the ancient snake oil salesmen of the 1800s, because Ranger standouts like Don "Bones" Raleigh, Pentti Lund, Frankie Eddolls, Neil Colville, and Zellio Toppazzini consumed the brew without question or hesitation. Which tells you more than you need to know about the shattered state of mind of the shaky New York Rangers at the time.

Well, hangovers to headaches, didn't that squad of swilling skaters proceed to go on a most unnatural—and unusual—winning streak! The Rangers won 10 of their next 12 games, and as each victory was penciled into the record book, more and more attention was being shifted toward this miraculous medicine that was taking the team to the top of the charts. More and more queries were being directed toward its mysterious contents. Leone insisted that the formula was a secret, but he did divulge the manner in which it was delivered.

The secret, Mr. Leone admitted, was that the secret elixir could be prepared only at the last minute to ensure its full power. He told the press, and everyone else who would listen since his restaurant was going great guns, that when the preparations were completed and the remedy was ready, it was given to Burchard. He would then board a plane with the miracle worker safely secured in a black bag, kept all warm and cozy and surrounded by a trio of hot water bottles that kept the concoction fresh and happy. There was still one special and all-important test left to prove the power of the potion.

The Rangers were about to embark on a true test of the mettle of the matter when they journeyed to Toronto to battle the Maple Leafs, a squad that always caused them pain, scorn, and any other noun you would like to insert. If Leone's elixir really was the real deal, it would have to make the Leafs fall.

Well, by this time, the whole thing had become a circus. Not since

Turk Broda was delegated to the fat farm had anything so novel put the game of hockey back on the front pages of the daily newspapers. Well, the Maple Leafs, always willing to play tag with the media, had a plan of their own. They arranged for Canada customs agents to seize the bottle. Since Burchard would not reveal its secret contents, the Leafs contended that the bottle could contain a lethal concoction or perhaps even a bomb.

However, Leone and Burchard had a few more allies in the Fifth Estate than the Leafs realized and they were clued in on the ploy. Burchard cleverly enticed a *Toronto Globe and Mail* photographer to distract the customs agent with a tasty selection (read bribe) of Christmas cigars and brandy while he slipped by, booty and all. Burchard rushed to Maple Leaf Gardens and arrived just in time to deliver the solution and have the lads drink the potion. Imagine the surprise on our entrepreneurs' faces when the Broadway boys went out and played like a team possessed. In the first seven minutes of period one, the lads pasted three pucks past Al Rollins and held on to post a 4–2 victory. It goes without saying, although I will say it anyway, full credit for the upset was attributed to Leone's Magic Elixir.

By this time, the rapid rise was becoming a rocket. Business at Leone's place was so brisk, he couldn't even find the time to concoct new batches of the stuff. Which was quickly becoming an issue, since everyone from scientists to doctors to religious quacks speculated on exactly what was in the Broadway bubbly. And really, here's where the boys start sinking their own ship.

When Leone announced he was going to sell his secret solution to the public, the vocal majority started chirping. Well, a sports team will use anything, real or imagined, to pull itself out of a slump. It was quite another thing for that special solution to be offered to Joe Public. Naysayers started spilling out of the woodwork. Some who choked back the syrupy sap said it reminded them of bad chicken soup on a very bad day. Others said it had the aroma of the Atlantic Ocean. Even some of the Rangers themselves said its bouquet was beyond their capacity to describe. And they were winning!

But some still believed. At least for a little while. But when Leone was too busy to deliver the "solution," the losses started to outnumber the wins. Even when the "elixir" did show up, it didn't seem to kick in. And quickly, the fad was dead. And so were the Rangers. They finished fifth, out of the playoffs and out of luck. So remember, there are no magic solutions to success; it's all hard work and good luck.

Where It All Started

When the "population-challenged" town of Kenora captured the Stanley Cup title in January 1907, some major city newspapers refused to acknowledge them as worthy champions. One of the most vocal deniers was the *Toronto Telegram*. But they didn't limit their editorial distaste to Kenora; they also had a healthy volley ready to fire on the village of Renfrew when that town issued its own request to wrestle for the Stanley Cup crown.

"And now Renfrew talks of challenging for the Stanley Cup," the newspaper reported on March 13, 1907, "and all because they have won a fence corner league and defeated a broken and discouraged band of Ottawas on Renfrew ice. Such a game would only help to show Renfrew's weakness to the world. If Renfrew had any real stars on her team, some of the big teams would have gobbled them up long ago, so further advertising is unnecessary."

Since those remarks raised a chuckle or two among the readers, the *Telegram* continued its scathing attack, this time slipping the satire a step farther and including the townsfolk in their biting remarks the following day: "Renfrew has challenged for the Stanley Cup. Now don't laugh. If you've never lived in a country town you don't know how seriously those people take themselves."

Angry words like those, from so aggressive an adversary, can carry considerable clout. So, it shouldn't be surprising that Renfrew was denied its Stanley Cup challenge in 1907. Just as it would be denied again in 1909. Now, this double slight from the big-city folks, with their big-time newspapers and their more-than-likely corrupt Stanley Cup trustees, festered in the mind-set of the folks of the town.

The powers that be decided there was only one thing that would make the garden green, and that was money. And, well, money talks.

And there were a lot of people who were listening in Renfrew, because big-time money was just around the corner.

A number of investors decided to compile a team of superstars that would be the envy of the entire hockey universe. Getting financing from local lumber baron Alexander Barnet in partnership with railroad builder/mining magnate M. J. O'Brien, manager Ambrose O'Brien lured future Hall-of-Fame members Cyclone Taylor, Newsy Lalonde, Frank Patrick, Lester Patrick, and Fred Whitcroft to play for the home side for the 1909–10 season.

The team, which would become known as the Renfrew Millionaires, was refused entry into the newly formed Canadian Hockey Association, as were the Montreal Wanderers. So, Montreal and Renfrew, along with Cobalt and Haileybury, decided to form their own league, which was dubbed the National Hockey Association. Within weeks, the CHA collapsed, and three of the doomed league's franchises joined the fledgling new NHA loop. Seven years later, the NHA would become the NHL, which is still the predominant professional hockey league on the planet.

As for Renfrew, despite their wealth of talent, they never did get to challenge for the Stanley Cup and in two years the club had folded, proving for the first—but hardly the last—time that money cannot buy championships.

And the rest—and the checks—is hockey history.

The Tiger

For someone like me, it couldn't have been more simple.
I fought—or I disappeared.

Dave "Tiger" Williams

"The Hammer" was a fierce competitor, but I never bit him in the cheek. I bit him on the nose because I was so damn mad at him at that particular moment. He's been one of the guys that I was able to meet after retiring and I'm glad I did. I don't know if two lawyers ever got in a room and had a toe-to-toe if they would ever talk to each other again, but with us guys, when it's over, we're just one of the boys again.

Dave "Tiger" Williams on the real NHL tough guy,
Dave Schultz

I would've preferred to play on the power play and score 50 goals a year like I did in junior hockey. When you're on a team, you've got to do what you can to make that team win as many games as possible. If you can do something better than the other guy, then you might as well be the guy to do it. You might not want to do it, but once you start being a checker, you'll be known as a checker your entire career.

Tiger Williams

He was and still is a real character, always willing to speak his mind and tell it the way he sees it. As strong and as mean as a bull, Tiger Williams was the last of a dying breed, the player who would go to any measure to back a teammate or go to any extreme to elevate his team to victory. He could fight and he could score. He was a complete package that you don't see very often anymore.

He got his name Tiger when he was a young kid because of his personality. When he came to the Leafs' training camp in '70, we all had heard about him as a draft pick, and a guy playing junior hockey and leading the Western Canadian Junior League in penalty minutes. When he first came to camp you could see the determination in him. Tiger had somewhat limited skills and his skating was something that he continually had to improve and work on. At that point in time, I don't think anybody thought that he would play in the National Hockey League for 15 years but he ended up having a very successful career.

Darryl Sittler

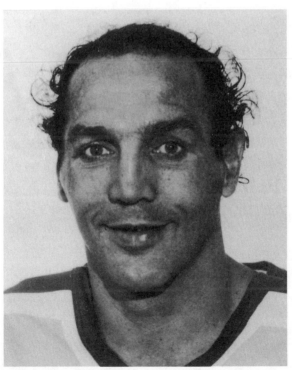

Tiger Williams remained—and remains—one of the game's great characters and character players.

When Tiger first joined the Toronto Maple Leafs, he noticed that Leafs' owner Harold Ballard would come into the dressing room and insult those players he considered to be "just lousy." When he asked a teammate about the Ballard fire and venom act, Tiger was told that Ballard didn't respect anyone who wouldn't stand up to him. Well, Williams wasn't exactly sure whether it was all just a gag or not, but when Ballard walked into the room one day and called Tiger a "little stubble-jumper from Saskatchewan," Tiger replied, "It's better than being a fat bastard from Ontario." After that, Ballard loved the fiery Williams and the Tiger always got along well with the boss.

Pound for pound, to me he was one of the toughest guys in the league. He was one of those players that came to play every night. He kept his own teammates honest, whether it was during practice or in the dressing room before the game, or just being ready to play. If you weren't, Tiger would put you in line. He also kept the opponents on their toes and honest as well.

Former Leafs coach Roger Neilson

Mark Messier—McArthur on Ice

Messier gives us the kind of enthusiasm and leadership, the clutch plays that we need. This is a great team we're playing against, and it's going to take a great team to beat them.

Glen Sather

It's an honor to be in the position to play on some great teams, and with some great players, not only on the team but as line mates. I've been involved with some great people. I guess I have to be thankful for that.

Mark Messier

Mark Messier would eventually become a storied captain and leader.

One day, Mario Lemieux, Wayne Gretzky, and Mark Messier all went up to heaven and they all met God at his throne. God asked them two questions.

God: Mario, what did you accomplish in your life?

Mario: Well, I won four scoring titles, two Stanley Cup championships, and after battling back from cancer, I led my team to the Eastern Conference finals.

God: And what did the people around think of you?

Mario: The people in Pittsburgh loved me!

God: Wayne, what did you accomplish in your life?

Wayne: Well, I won ten NHL scoring titles, I was named as the league's MVP nine times, I collected five Lady Byng Trophies, earned five Lester B. Pearson Awards, and I helped lead the Edmonton Oilers to four Stanley Cup championships.

God: And what did the people around think of you?

Wayne: The people of North America loved me so much they called me the Great One!

God: Goodness, the Great One? Well. Okay, Mark, what did you accomplish in your life?

Mark: Well, I reached the 50-goal mark once, the 100-point plateau five times. I was named the 1984 playoff MVP and I had my name etched in on the Stanley Cup five times with Edmonton and once with the New York Rangers. In the 1993–94 playoffs, I promised—actually guaranteed—that the Rangers would win game six of the Eastern

Conference finals, and then I went out and scored three goals to make good on my promise. Then I went and delivered a Stanley Cup title to the fans on Broadway.

God: And what did the people around think of you?

Mark: Well, the people in New York love me, and frankly, they think you're sitting in *my* seat!

Mark is an inspiration to play with. He plays so hard and always seems to come up with the big play when we need it most. Being on the same line with him, all you can do is try to work hard and keep up with him.

New York Rangers teammate Adam Graves

I was fighting back tears, so I could only imagine what Mark was going through. You really feel what Mark meant to the city and what the city meant to him. How could anyone watch that and not feel emotional? He brought their team the Stanley Cup. Thank God he's on our team now.

Dave Scatchard on Messier's first game at Madison Square Garden as a member of the Canucks

When I left here I left everything here. It's time to move on.

Mark Messier

Gilles Gratton with his famous snarling tiger mask

TRUE FLAKES WHO TAKE THE CAKE

Grattoony the Loony

Gilles Gratton was one of hockey's more unique and offbeat specimens. Since he was a goaltender, he was already half-a-bubble shy of plumb as it was. But Grattoony the Loony had a few other marbles that were loose. He played the piano before games to relax, which isn't all that odd until you realized he didn't have a clue how to play the instrument and the accompanying racket was anything but soothing. But that was just the tip of the iceberg. Gratton believed he had been a Spanish conquistador in a previous lifetime and once admitted he couldn't play a game because of the injuries he had suffered during one of his glorious battles.

Former minor league trainer and NHL goaltender Les Binkley, who had a few yarns of his own to string along, played with Gratton in the old WHA. "I remember one night when we were in Chicago," Binkley recalled, "we sat next to each other in the locker room strapping on our pads when he suddenly asked me: 'What city are we in?' I said, 'Chicago.' He paused and replied, 'Did you know, Mars is crossing Jupiter tonight? I shouldn't be here. I can't play here tonight.' And he didn't play that game."

And then there was Grattoony's infamous "dead fish" routine. After making a good save—which wasn't all that often—Gratton would just drop to the ice as if he had been shot. The team trainer would scurry onto the ice and hustle over to the fallen goalkeeper. When he reached him, Gratton would look up, smile, and ask about the fan reaction. "Did they like it? How did it compare with other dives?" he would ask. By the time the trainer had returned to the bench, the entire team would be rolling in the aisle behind the bench.

John Kordic

Not a Pretty Picture

O ne of the most tortured players—both emotionally and physically—to ever skate in the NHL was enforcer turned maniac John Kordic, who had the right combination of offensive skill, intimidation, and courage to have become a player like Chris Simon. But John was thrown into the fray as a tough guy, and with his chiseled physique and powerful punches, it became a role he was forced to play throughout his career.

While Kordic was with the Maple Leafs, he had a rather tempestuous relationship with winger Gary Leeman, whom John considered to be a phony. The fact that Leeman was also carrying on a not-so-secret clandestine relationship with another player's wife made him the subject of

John Kordic

trade rumors and cheap humor. Nothing upset Kordic more than unrest and distrust in the dressing room. For all his faults, John was a true believer in the old credo—what happened in the room, stayed in the room, and was settled in the room. Rumor had it that he settled a "maleficence" or two in his own way and in his own court of law.

Whenever the Leafs returned from a road trip, Kordic always hired a limo to pick him up and drive him home. Many of the other players depended on their wives or better halves to serve as chaperones, or they left their own cars at the airport. One evening, the club arrived back in Toronto after a road excursion to Chicago, only to find the city in a deep freeze with record low temperatures. Many of the players were stranded in the parking lot, subjected to subzero weather and deader-than-a doornail car batteries. Not John, no way. His limousine was there and waiting, cozy and comfortable. He made the driver survey the lot until he spotted a shivering Gary Leeman standing beside his isolated automobile. Kordic had the driver creep up beside the exasperated Leeman and stop. When Leeman spotted the car, he assumed Kordic was either going to offer him a boost or a drive into the city. Kordic ordered the driver to pause until Leeman was right beside the car. Then, he rolled down the window and said, "See ya later, scumbag," and had the driver floor it, leaving a shivering and jilted Leeman shuffling in the cold.

Wild Thing

A l Iafrate always marched to the beat of a different drummer. On the ice, he possessed one of the hardest slap shots of any player to ever dent the boards and one of the oddest heads of hair ever seen by spectators and players alike. Not that it was seen all that often, since Al rarely doffed his bonnet. Even during the playing of the national anthems, Al's helmet stayed securely in place. But those who did get a glimpse of the Iafrate lid described it as a raccoon on steroids, whatever that means. Off the ice, he smoked like a chimney, drove like a bandit, and had a wide and varied collection of "hogs": huge souped-up Harley-Davidson motorcycles. And he was always loved by his teammates, no matter where he played.

One night in Philadelphia, while the Wild Thing was playing for Washington, Flyers' winger Claude Boivin nailed Iafrate behind the net, driving him with considerable force into the end glass. Iafrate got up, cleared the cobwebs from his head, and began skating hard to deliver a retaliatory strike against Boivin. What the Wild One didn't know, but what most of the spectators realized, was that the force of Boivin's hit had broken the belt Iafrate used to keep his hockey pants in place.

Well, Al wasn't a "suspenders" guy. For Big Al, it was the belt way or no way. That was all well and good, until this particular evening at least. After being decked by Boivin, Big Al went on the warpath, looking to wreak havoc and seek revenge. But when he started skating, his momentum caused his pants to flop to his knees, which caused him to sputter and spin until he tripped. When he did, he treated one side of the arena to the extremely rare "indoor full moon." When Big Al realized the state of his undress, he was still 40 feet from the bench. By the time he crawled over there, the whole arena was aware of his predicament and he was greeted with an assortment of wiseass remarks that are best not repeated here. That was Al Iafrate, and he is missed.

The Missing Link

In the first round we drafted Mike Modano to protect the franchise, in the second round we drafted Link Gaetz to protect Mike, and in the third round we should've drafted a lawyer to protect Link.
Former Minnesota North Stars general manager Lou Nanne

Let's face it. The NHL has always employed its fair share of loose-lipped, mentally shaky, off-the-cuff individuals who, if judged by their behavior on the ice, may have had a hard time finding employment in a "normal" outside world. Yet, many of the zaniest on-ice characters are nothing more than calm kittens off the ice. "Missing Link" Gaetz does not fall into that category.

Link was a hard-hitting, in-your-face competitor with a hammer for a fist and an anvil for a chin. He could outslug anyone on the ice and tried to outslug everyone off the ice. By the time he made it to the NHL with the North Stars in 1988–89, he was known for two things: his battles with the opposition on the ice and his battles with the bottle off the ice. It wasn't until he tried to throw a television through the door of his hotel room—while the door was still closed—that management realized he had a bit of a problem. But Link loved the game and he continued to play wherever he could—including a stint with an outfit called the Mexico City Toroeos. It seemed there was always another circuit out there somewhere waiting to sign him. There are too many Gaetz tales to recount here, but a couple of his recent excursions will give you an idea as to the nature of our protagonist's shaky psyche.

Many thought Link was really missing something when he signed a contract in February 1998 to suit up with the Miramichi Leafs of the Northumberland Senior Hockey League in New Brunswick. While he was in the salmon fishing capital of Canada, Link caused quite a stir on and off the ice. All went fairly smoothly until the playoffs. In the New Brunswick senior league, a player is automatically ejected after one fight, so the Miramichi coach had to use his "trump" card judiciously— if at all. The Miramichi Leafs were a team that was put together with only one goal in mind—to advance to the Allan Cup tournament. The coaches couldn't afford to have their Gaetz swinging open and taking ill-timed penalties, so they nailed him to the pine for much of the play-offs. Sitting did not sit well with Mr. Gaetz. During the second game of the Leafs' semifinal series against Truro, Gaetz left the bench midway through the second period, walked into the dressing room, tore off his uniform, and walked out on the team, never to return. The folks in northern New Brunswick were the fortunate ones. The good old boys of Texas weren't so lucky.

Link Gaetz

In January 1999, Gaetz was detained in Texas on charges of public intoxication and resisting arrest. Police were summoned to a disturbance call at an apartment complex, where they found the no-longer-missing Gaetz. When the cops tried to restrain him, he fought with the officers. When he was arraigned at the local courthouse, Link cursed and swore at Walker County Court-at-Law Judge Barbara Hale. Then, in typical Link-fashion, he made the judge an offer that even she couldn't refuse. "I told Mr. Gaetz that his bond would be set at $10,000," Judge Hale recounted later. "He replied, 'Well hell, make it $100,000,' so I did."

Well, Link was exonerated and exited that tempest in a Texas teapot. He first thought to take a break from hockey and work in Alaska, but instead he joined the Eston Ramblers, a senior outfit that plays in the Saskatchewan Wild Goose League. They say you can teach an old dog new tricks, but apparently you can't teach him much. In his first game, he received a league record 68 penalty minutes in one shift. Apparently you are thrown out of the game after one fight, so Link decided to get his money's worth and fight anyone he could get his hands on.

Word on the street has it that Link is recovering and doing well, but he no longer plays the game he loved so much.

The Kindred Spirit

My job is to get my shoulder into somebody.

Howie Young

He had a lot of talent. Howie was very strong, a good skater who could shoot the puck. But he didn't seem to have it mentally.

Norm Ullman

On January 28, 1963, the bible of all sports magazines, *Sports Illustrated,* released its weekly issue with a picture of a handsome, well-sculpted athlete named Howie Young on the cover. A defenseman with the Detroit Red Wings, Young was a rambunctious, free-wheeling fireball whose main claim to fame was that he could and would capsize, crunch, and pulverize anyone who came near the Wings' holy trinity of Gordie Howe, Alex Delvecchio, and Normie Ullman. Now, all three of these men were more than capable of taking care of themselves, but a new dynamic was being introduced into the NHL: the policemen. These were players whose main role was to be on patrol and cuff any perpetrator who dared stroll into the path of the team's biggest stars. Mr. Young was very effective in his duties. Unfortunately, like the aforementioned Mr. Gaetz, he also had a weakness for the blessings of the bottle.

On the bench I would say, "Please God, just get me through this game." Then it was, "Hey, God, just get me through this period." Finally, it was, "God, just get me through this shift."

Howie Young

Before he even made that storied appearance on the cover of *Sports Illustrated*, Howie Young was well known, mainly for his antics and his over-the-top, under-the-wall behavior. In 1962, the Hamilton Tiger Cubs, Young's former junior club, were playing the Edmonton Oil Kings for the Memorial Cup championship, Canada's top junior hockey prize. At this time, Young was a member of the Western Hockey League's Edmonton Flyers, the top minor league farm club of the Detroit Red Wings, who just happened to be Mr. Young's employers. Even though his

Howie Young

"alma mater" was playing, Young decided to toe the party line and throw his support behind the Oil Kings. He showed up one evening with a healthy glow on, decked out in full cowboy regalia, complete with cowboy boots and a 10-gallon Stetson. All was well, until our little daredevil (he would go on to become a successful movie stuntman) decided to take a walk on the wild side. He climbed up onto the ledge of the dasher boards surrounding the ice surface and step-danced his way around the entire rink, whirling his hat in the air and leading all the Edmonton fans gathered there in a regaling cheer.

Well, Eddie Bush, the Hamilton Tiger Cubs' coach, was not amused. He insisted a member of the local constabulary take Mr. Young into custody. When the officer appointed to perform that duty attempted to remove Mr. Young from his perch, Howie delivered a howitzer, knocking the cop colder than a tomb.

Many of the newspapers the next day featured a picture of a grinning Howie Young, cowboy hat in hand, waving wildly to the appreciative crowd while perilously perched on the dasher. He was oblivious to the storm of policemen barely seen in the background who were preparing to snatch their match and escort him to the "crowbar" hotel.

After the Red Wings soured on his act, he was traded to the Los Angeles Blades of the Western Hockey League. Believe it or not, his on-ice antics caught the attention of a talent agent who believed Young could be an actor. The agent arranged a screen test for the fledgling star and before you know it, Young had landed a part as a U.S. Marine in the 1965 Frank Sinatra World War Two opus, *None But the Brave.* His performance on-screen was surprisingly true and strong, but his actions off the set were commonplace and ordinary. In July 1965, he was arrested for breaking into his own apartment. It was on that night, sitting alone and dejected, lost and afraid, in a jail cell in downtown Los Angeles, that Howie Young decided to leave the life of liquor and return to the land of the living. Two days later he joined Alcoholics Anonymous, and according to everyone who knew him, he remained sober for the rest of his life.

He never gave up the dream of playing hockey, however, and he continued to search out employment wherever it might be found, whether it was the World Hockey Association, the Central Hockey League, or the short-lived Pacific Hockey League. For Howie, life on the ice just seemed nice.

After the demise of the WHA and the birth of Wayne Gretzky, minor league hockey in the USA took a serious nosedive. Howie continued to find steady employment as a rodeo cowboy and a movie stuntman, but he still had the nagging urge to play the only game he truly loved.

In 1985, at the age of 48, he attempted a comeback in both the IHL and NAHL. He never explained why he would put himself through what ultimately would be a losing proposition. The thing was, he didn't do too badly. It's just that neither team was willing to give up a roster spot to an "old-timer" when a kid could do the same job, at the same wage, without the worries. By this time, Young had moved to Thoreau, New Mexico, a predominantly Navajo community two hours west of Albuquerque. It was there that he became a mentor to a bunch of Indian kids who thought "Howe" was nothing more than a white man's greeting and Orr was a paddle everyone needed to propel his canoe down the river. His dream was to produce the NHL's first Navajo player. "These kids are such natural athletes," he once said, "all I've got to do is bring the ice, and they'll do the rest."

Someone else will have to carry on his vision. Howie Young died on November 24, 1999. He was 62 years old.

Voices from the Gondola and Beyond

He shoots, he scores.

Foster Hewitt

Henderson has scored for Canada.

Foster Hewitt

Hitler sits the blueline.

Brian McFarlane

It appears Risebrough has pugnaciously construed that check and will undoubtedly make a visitation to the box of punition.

Danny Gallivan

Lafleur rather gingerly up to Lemaire, Lemaire crosses the line, back to Lafleur, he scores!

Danny Gallivan's call on the goal that crushed Boston and catapulted the Canadiens toward their fourth straight Stanley Cup victory

Mayday, Mayday, Mayday.

Rick Jeanneret

They're really trying to score now.

Bob Cole

It . . . is . . . over!

Paul Romaniuk

Good night, nurse.

Joe Bowen

Down goes Brown.

Joe Bowen

Holy Mackinaw.

Joe Bowen

Do you believe in miracles?

Al Michaels

How would you like this guy operating on you with those hands when he missed an open net in the semifinals between Edmonton and Chicago?

Don Cherry on Randy Carlyle, who was planning on attending medical school

"He shoots! He scores!" Those four words made Foster Hewitt a hockey legend. "I can't really remember how it happened," Hewitt recalled when asked how he coined his most famous phrase. "Suddenly there was a player moving in on (Kitchener goalie George) Hainsworth and his shot fell behind the frustrated goalie. I described it in those four words. It stayed with me ever since."

When the Toronto Maple Leafs went on the road in the old days, they were usually greeted by hundreds of fans gathered at the train station to meet the team. More often than not, the person those fans were waiting to see and grab an autograph from wasn't Conacher or Clancy or Kennedy. Those fans wanted to see and hear Foster Hewitt. It was his voice that brought the thrills and chills of the world's fastest game into their living rooms, and he was a real star.

One of the most popular play-by-play announcers currently spreading hockey's gospel on the airwaves is Joe Bowen, today's voice of the Leafs.

"I dearly love what I'm doing," said Bowen, who handles midweek Leafs telecasts and broadcasts weekend games on radio. "It's the greatest job in the world and I pinch myself regularly to make sure I know it is that. I tried working once at the 5,000-foot level [in a nickel mine for] Inco and I didn't like that very much. I'd like to do this as long as I can. It's too much fun to give up."

His catch phrases include: "tonight's keepers of the hempen huts," "the couriers of the corded cottage," "Good night, nurse," and his most famous marker, "Holy Mackinaw." It's a safe bet that at some point during a game, Bowen will use his signature call at least once.

"It's funny," Bowen related recently, "my dad used to say that every once in a while, and one night I was doing a game with (former agent, analyst, and currently Leaf assistant general manager) Bill Watters and something spectacular happened and that blurted out of my mouth. I used it again a couple of times and then all of a sudden it became a little bit of a signature."

One Night Stand

He played only one game in the National Hockey League. One game! Yet, he is more famous than most everyone who wore an NHL uniform, he makes more money than most of today's superstars, and his opinions/suggestions/lectures are regarded as gospel by that faction of fans who treat the game as a religion. He is Donald S. Cherry, his pulpit is a cramped TV set located in downtown Toronto, and his word is as pure as the Lord's law.

Oh, don't get me wrong, Don played the game. He played it with a passion and a desire that only exists in whimsical novels today. But he didn't make the show, except for that one glorious night during the 1955 Stanley Cup semifinals. And what a night it was. Trust Mr. Cherry to make a debut unlike any other.

In 1955, Don Cherry was called up from the minors by the Boston Bruins to replace the injured Fern Flaman in what turned out to be the final game of the key playoff match-up against the Montreal Canadiens at the Forum. To make the event even more memorable, Grapes was in the starting lineup. It was also the game in which the Canadiens decided to honor their suspended superstar, Maurice "Rocket" Richard. You can imagine the apprehension Grapes was feeling, having to stand there toeing the blueline while 17,000 fans went wild and gave the Rocket a lengthy standing ovation.

One of Cherry's teammates that evening was Hal Laycoe, the former Canadien whose hair the Rocket had combed and parted with his stick, which helped earn Richard a seat on the sidelines for the entire play-offs. Laycoe was particularly upset by the display of love and loyalty that the fans thrust upon the Rocket. Throw a 5–1 season-ending loss on the pyre and the result was a Laycoe explosion that tore the dressing room apart. At the time, Cherry was certain that he would see lots more moments like that one, but it wasn't to be. He injured his knee in an off-season softball game and wasn't in top form at training camp that fall. He was relegated to the minors, where he played for another 16 years. When he finally did get back to an NHL arena it was as the coach of the Boston Bruins.

Behind the Pine

The remedy, right now, is two scotches and an aspirin, I think.

Bruins general manager Harry Sinden after his team was eliminated from the playoffs

If you show up five minutes after the store doors open, they are in a Blues uniform.

Former New York Ranger general manager Neil Smith on the spending habits of the St. Louis Blues

It hit me like one of Joe Frazier's left hooks, I felt like Dr. Richard Kimble. I felt like for all these years, I've been chasing the one-armed man, and I finally caught him, and it turned out to be the wrong guy.

Tommy McVie on not being hired as the next Bruins head coach

Then I had to speak. It wasn't easy at all, but there were things I wanted to say. I said that, when they honored me, they honored not only me, but Clancy and all the old guard of players, the ones who won the games. I said that if I ever took another hockey job I hoped I would be fortunate enough to have men like them playing for me. I said I wouldn't have missed it for the world the years I'd spent managing and coaching the Leafs, especially the four years we'd won the Stanley Cup. It might be the end of an era, I said, but one thing about that era—it had never been dull.

Punch Imlach, April 23, 1969, after being released by the Leafs

He was deadly against anyone placing a hat on the bed. He also hated two-dollar bills to the point that when he won a $200 bet from a friend and the fellow paid him off in 100 two-dollar bills, he tore them all up and threw them on the dressing-room floor.

Famed sports writer George Gross on Punch Imlach

What I find exciting is that we're down to the end of the season and we're still playing. It's like Jack Nicklaus always said—all you can ask for is to be in a position to win. You can't predict victory, but it is a terrific feeling to get close. It's sort of like Christmas. You know it is coming, but it's the beginning of December and you take it in stride. When it gets to be December 23, you feel all the excitement, all the emotions. I guess that's how I feel now—like this is Christmas.

Scotty Bowman on the thrill of coaching in the Stanley Cup playoffs

His competence as a coach means he can read his team and adapt to his players—although his players know they must adapt to him even more. He knows how to "read" his players— to determine their moods, quirks, and tendencies, getting to know them and what motivates them and what doesn't. Some players need a push, some need a different level of support.

Mike Keenan on Scotty Bowman, *The Sporting News*, November 24, 2000

One of the tactics that coaches do use is to employ more physical players, and sometimes that results in more physical confrontation between players that do fight. But not necessarily does it always result in fisticuffs; it may be just a tactic that a coach will use to offset or develop a swing in momentum, which is a big part of the game of hockey.

Former Boston Bruins coach Mike Keenan

I took the corporate bicycle up and down Long Island to sign this player. Unlike my neighbors, the corporate jet wasn't available.

Mike Milbury on the signing of Chris Ferraro and his New York Ranger neighbors

This isn't microbiology. I've been in the game 16 years and should have figured out something.

Mike Milbury on winning Coach of the Year

He's very brainy but sometimes, he thinks so much that his plate overheats and it causes interference in our earphones during games.

Marc Crawford on Scotty Bowman, May 24, 1996

I kept telling Marc, "I told you last year; I don't have a plate in my head." I told him, "I knew your father before you did. And I don't think he would be too proud of you right now."

Scotty Bowman on Marc Crawford, May 25, 1996

Lose a game in this town and everyone wants to put bullets in the boat. You guys (media) think this is easy.

Pat Quinn, Toronto Maple Leafs head coach

Hard as Nails

I figured, if I wasn't playing hockey, I was going to die.

John Brophy

They don't make them like John Brophy anymore. A career minor-leaguer, Broph was mean, lean, and never clean and he never backed down from anyone or anything. He was hard as nails, tough as tar paper, and willing to tackle any sailor who dared bring his ship into the Brophy zone.

Brophy spent the majority of his career in the old Eastern Hockey League with the Long Island Ducks. The EHL was a league where courage outweighed charisma and guts outbid grit. The Ducks played out on Veterans Highway from 1959 through the end of the 1973 season. That was long before anyone had ever heard of guys like Bryan Trottier, Mike Bossy, or Bobby Nystrom and long before NHL wannabe's like the New York Islanders and the New Jersey Devils settled into the swamps of New Jersey and the industrial parks of Long Island.

In the 1960s, the people's choice was a guy from Nova Scotia, Canada, named John Brophy. His face was creased with a wide array of swaths that made his mug look like a map of railroad tracks. He sported a military-styled buzz cut that made every hair seem as sharp as a spike and appear to be the color of cold steel.

I certainly don't try to coach a player to play the way I played. I wouldn't expect a player to try to do the kind of things I was trying to do. You have to be a certain kind of player to do that. Nobody was going to take away from me what I had. I played as if my life depended on it.

John Brophy

Just how tough was John Brophy? Well, during the summer of 1967, he was in a serious automobile accident, suffered a fractured skull, received at least 375 stitches, and was still ready to start the season. And then there were the "games" against New Haven, which were little more than excuses for hand-to-hand combat. One night the Ducks were in New Haven doing battle with the Blades, and as usual, all kinds of crazy things were happening out there. Brophy was being stitched over the eye in the home dressing room when another brawl broke out back on the ice. Broph raced back onto the ice with the needle and thread still in his face. Two days later, New Haven visited Long Island. There was a promotion going on called Kids Afternoon. The stands were packed to the rafters and even the local television station was on hand. "We came out and a fight broke out before the teams even finished their warm-up skate," Brophy recalled. "We would play for 40 seconds and then fight for 40 minutes. So, after this goes on for a while, the New Haven guys just get on the bus and go home. They left everybody just standing there."

When that big guy comes bearing down on you, you start looking over your shoulder. He makes you think about him instead of your job.

Norm Ryder, the New Haven player traded for Brophy

In 1968, Brophy was traded to New Haven in one of the biggest blockbuster trades in EHL history. That was akin to Willie Mays's going from the New York Giants to the Brooklyn Dodgers. The fact that John had spent the previous season on the pine for slipping a butt end into a referee's ribs and was suspended for the rest of the year may have played a part in the decision to send him down the coast. Of course, it must also be noted that Broph was soon behind the pine, taking over as skipper of the Ducks when it was apparent that the EHL brass wasn't going to cut him any slack. In Brophy's first game back on Long Island, one of the fans who only days earlier were bemoaning Brophy's being dispatched to such an archrival like New Haven, crowned Broph with a bottle to the back of his head. Broph understood. Rivals are rivals. The same fan was back on his feet and cheering a year later when Brophy was traded back to the Ducks. So, at least for John Brophy, you can go home again.

Despite his fiery, often volatile on-ice temper, Brophy was able to settle quite efficiently into the role of bench boss. He went on to coach in a whole universe of leagues, from the EHL to the SHL to the WHA to the AHL, and finally made it to the show with the Toronto Maple Leafs from 1986 to 1988. After his stint with the Leafs, Broph made a permanent home for himself as the bench boss of the Hampton Road Admirals. Along the way he became the most successful coach in the history of the ECHL.

The European Angle

L arry Huras played two games in the NHL. Most record books only have him playing a single contest, but Huras knew better. He was well aware that he suited up twice and he knew that he saw the ice on both nights. He wrote the offices of the NHL Official Guide and Record Book and asked them to check into his claim. A check of the official NHL game sheets proved the man right. He did play in two games with the New York Rangers in the 1976–77 season. It may seem to be a petty matter, but it is not. When almost all of the official hockey guides have you disappearing from the face of the hockey map after the 1979–80 season when you actually played top-level hockey until 1993–94, you tend to become a tad defensive about your rightful place on the hockey highway. And that's what Huras was, a hardworking, gritty defenseman who played and coached in the professional leagues of France for 13 seasons after his North American dreams had been erased.

Huras is a soft-spoken, kind, and friendly sort who is intensely proud of his contribution to the game of hockey in Europe. Many former NHL players who continued their careers in Europe tend to ignore or even deny that they played overseas. That is not the case with Larry Huras. He is one of the rare souls who appreciate the sport of hockey for what it really is—a game of skill, courage, and speed. Regardless of where it is played or the level it is played at, it can still mesmerize and amaze, just by the sheer beauty of its pace and the dexterity of its athletes.

As a player in France, he helped lead Grenoble to a pair of championships and, later, as a playing coach, he guided HC Rouen to four league championships and two berths in the European Cup finals. In 2000–1, Huras took over the reins of the ZSC Zurich franchise in the Swiss National League. He has a deep love for his sport, and he is not afraid to spread his gospel for the improvement of the sport.

"The Stanley Cup finals are still one of the best shows going but during the regular season, I would much rather watch one of our Swiss league games," Huras admits; "there is more flow to it and a bigger emphasis is placed on the skill part of the game."

And like many pundits he realizes that while the game has grown bigger, better, and bulkier, the NHL has not adapted to that increase in size. "In the NHL, there isn't any room to make any plays," Huras says. "To improve the quality of play they should remove the center ice red line to open up the neutral zone and eventually expand to European-size ice surfaces (30 x 60 meters as opposed to 26 x 56–58 meters) or play four against four ice hockey."

"There is a mind-set in the NHL that if they change the red line rule as we have in Europe, that teams will stop forechecking leading to even more trapping in the neutral zone. Teams still forecheck successfully in all the leagues over here but you have to make good decisions and read the game and situation well."

Huras hopes to be able to bring those ideas back across the pond and instill them in the mind-set of the NHL. If he continues to have success as a coach in Europe, perhaps he'll be patrolling the bench as an NHL skipper in the near future.

To Serve and Protect

In the mid-1960s, the Montreal Canadiens went in search of a tough forward who could protect the team's star players, like Henri Richard, Yvan Cournoyer, and Jean Beliveau. The NHL was changing. Previously, players fought their own battles, and they didn't need anyone to back them up. Gordie Howe, Maurice Richard, and Ted Lindsay took on all comers. Even Jean Beliveau, who is still known as one of the most gentlemanly players to ever wear an NHL jersey, set a Montreal team record for the most penalty minutes in a season in the same year he won his first scoring title. He didn't get challenged too often after that. When Frank Mahovlich was gunning for 50 goals in 1960–61, he once challenged the entire Montreal Canadiens bench to a fight. The Habs bench got a pretty good laugh out of Mahovlich's offer, but it also gained the big guy a measure of respect. The Big M missed the 50-goal plateau that year, perhaps because he spent over 130 minutes in the sin bin for fighting his own battles. Mahovlich never reached triple digits in penalty minutes again.

At the conclusion of the 1962–63 season, the Habs' brass had a sit-down and discussed what the team needed to do for them to make a return to the Stanley Cup winner's circle. One of those needs addressed by the Canadiens was the team's lack of an efficient on-ice cop. With Tom Johnson gone to Boston, Doug Harvey dispatched to New York, and Dickie Moore lost to retirement, the Habs' once mighty roster was now merely meek and mild. One of their scouts figured the man they needed was on the roster of the AHL's Cleveland Barons and he was available.

The fellow's name was John Ferguson, he was tough as they come, and he could score, as evidenced by the 38 goals and 177 penalty minutes he racked up in 1962–63. There was another item the scout mentioned that brought a smile to the faces of the Montreal management. He told the story of how Ferguson was skating around, firing a few slappers during the pregame warm-up. He noticed one of his Cleveland teammates chatting with a member of the Rochester Americans, the Barons' opponents that evening. Fergie grabbed a puck and drilled a slap shot that hit his own teammate flush on the back of his leg. When he skated over to him, it wasn't to apologize—it was to deliver a stern lecture about fraternizing with a member of the other team.

How far did Ferguson take his distaste for affiliating with members of the opposition? It was commonplace for Fergie to leave a just-served, expensive, and tasty full meal sitting on the table if a player from another team entered the restaurant that he happened to be dining in. One teammate was known to have said that he could have lived on the meal money Fergie tossed away in disgust. Ferguson went on to play eight seasons with the Habs, helping them win five Stanley Cup titles with a closed fist and a quick wrist.

A Different Kind of Stick Swinging

Hockey and golf have always gone together. Many of the same skills are required to excel at both games and the seasons complement one another. Many hockey players are excellent golfers and numerous charity golf tournaments staged by NHL players take place every summer. Goaltender Grant Fuhr has played in Q-schools, Mario Lemieux has mused about becoming a golf pro, and former NHL journeyman Dan Quinn is a leading money winner on the celebrity golf tour. But one NHLer—and a tough guy at that—actually made the jump to the PGA and enjoyed some success. "Wild Bill" Ezinicki, who played with Toronto, Boston, and New York, retired from hockey in 1955 to become a pro golfer. While on the PGA tour, he finished second at the Bob Hope Classic and fourth at the New Orleans Open.

NOT-SO-FAMOUS FIRSTS

The Slickest Swede

The first European-trained player to make it to the NHL was Ulf Sterner, who was a standout at the 1963 World Championships. He impressed the New York Ranger scouts in attendance so much that they invited him to attend the New York Rangers training camp in September 1963. Sterner actually attended the camp and earned a five-game NHL trial, but the IIHF threatened to strip him of his amateur status if he played in a professional game. It wasn't until after the 1964 Olympics that Sterner was able to fulfill his dream of playing in North America.

Sterner attended the Rangers' training camp again in 1964 and was assigned to the club's main AHL farm team in Baltimore. Although he had some early success, the experience was an unpleasant one for Sterner. He was under constant media scrutiny and often on the wrong end of a high stick from his opponents. Although he was productive, collecting 44 points in 52 games, he was also benched for indifferent play and eventually Sterner was sent down a peg to St. Paul of the Central Hockey League. He did see action in four games with the Rangers, but his ice time was limited. At the conclusion of the season, he returned to Sweden and signed to play with Rogle Angelhorn, a Division II team in the Swedish Elite League.

From Behind the Curtain

The first player from behind the Iron Curtain to reach the NHL was a Czechoslovakian-born rightwinger named Jaroslav Jirik. A veteran of three Olympic Game tournaments and a member of the Czech National Team for 12 years, Jirik was granted permission by Czechoslovakian authorities to leave Europe and play a season in North America. He signed with the St. Louis Blues and spent the season with Kansas City of the CHL, collecting 19 goals and 16 assists. After Kansas City failed to make the playoffs, Jirik was promoted to the Blues and appeared in three games against Chicago, Los Angeles, and Oakland. Although he was invited to attend the Blues' training camp prior to the 1970–71 season, Jirik was denied permission to return to North America. He had married an American woman while he was in the USA, and the Czech authorities felt if he returned, he would most certainly defect. But since he realized he probably wouldn't have made the NHL squad anyway, Jirik was content to remain in Czechoslovakia and play for his club team in Brno as well as the Czech national team. A second Czech, Jarda Krupicka, a native of Brno, Czechoslovakia, played with the New York Raiders and Los Angeles Sharks of the WHA in 1972–73.

From Russia for Love

The first Russian-trained athlete to play in the NHL was Victor Nechaev and his story is filled with enough political intrigue and behind-the-scenes conspiracy to fill a Robert Ludlum spy novel. Nechaev wasn't exactly a superstar in Russia, and he spent most of his playing time with the SKA Leningrad team. In 1981, Nechaev met an American student who was traveling through the Soviet Union named Cheryl Haigler. Despite cultural and language differences, they had a whirlwind romance and were married. She returned to the USA when her visa expired but it took Nechaev several months to obtain his "release" from the Soviet officials. Yet, instead of going to Boston where his wife was living, he moved to Los Angeles, where his cousin ran a Russian-language TV and radio station. There were rumors and innuendoes about Nechaev's sexual preferences and whether his marriage was nothing more than a clever device to get him out of Russia and into America. Regardless, Nechaev went Hollywood in Los Angeles instead of going colonial in Massachusetts.

When he arrived on the left coast, Nechaev met Los Angeles Kings general manager George Maguire and asked for a tryout. Maguire found a pair of skates, gave the Russian prospect a quick look-see, and was impressed enough to select him in the 1982 draft. Nechaev showed promise in training camp and earned a berth with the New Haven Nighthawks of the AHL where he registered 11 points in 28 games. He also appeared in three games for the Kings, scoring his first—and only—NHL goal. From all reports he was a contentious fellow, and when he balked at returning to the minors after his brief tour of duty with the Kings, he was released.

The Man Who Was But Never Was

The first player selected in the Amateur Draft who didn't exist was Taro Tsujimoto. While Mr. Tsujimoto was a real person, it's doubtful he ever slipped on the blades and took a spin around the ice surfaces near his home in Buffalo. In the early days of the draft, teams could use another team's pick if that team didn't care to make a selection. Punch Imlach's authoritarian attitude wouldn't allow him to let any team take advantage of his generosity, so Mr. Tsujimoto was selected 183rd overall by Buffalo in the 1973 Amateur Draft. And who was Taro Tsujimoto? No one really knows; it was just the name of a Japanese-American that Imlach lifted from the Buffalo phone book.

School for Scandal

The first college-trained head coach in NHL history was Ned Harkness, who briefly handled the reins of the Detroit Red Wings during the 1970–71 season. Although he was born in Canada, Harkness became an American citizen in 1949 and then embarked on one of the most successful university careers in U.S. college hockey history. In 1950, he founded the varsity hockey program in Troy at New York's Rensselaer Polytechnic Institute (RPI) and guided the Engineers to their first NCAA championship in 1954. In 1963, Harkness took over the coaching reins at Cornell University and led the team to a pair of NCAA titles in 1967 and 1970. The 1970 championship team finished the season with a 29-0-0 record, a NCAA Division I hockey mark that will probably never be eclipsed.

In 1970, Harkness became the first coach to go directly from the American college ranks to the NHL when he was appointed the new bench boss of the Detroit Red Wings. Unfortunately, it was not an easy transition for the scholarly Harkness. After only 38 games behind the bench, the Wings were floundering near the bottom of the NHL pool with a 12-22-4 record and hordes of angry fans were demanding that Harkness be dismissed. Well, exactly the opposite occurred because Red Wings' boss Bruce Norris did the unthinkable. Instead of firing Harkness, he promoted him to general manager, ousting Sid Abel from the office he had held for decades and terminating the Hall-of-Fame member's 31-year association with the Motown team.

From there, the Red Wings began a hasty downward spiral, missing the playoffs in 11 of the next 12 seasons. Much of the blame for the demise can be directed at the "Silver Shovels"—the executives who operated the front office under Norris's ownership. Harkness himself must also take his share of the shame. After all, he hired Ted Garvin to coach the club, which led to one of the more interesting evenings ever witnessed at the old Olympia. Garvin had no NHL experience, although he did have a pretty good track record in the IHL. His tenure with the Red Wings was alarmingly brief. After the club opened the 1973–74 season with only two wins in 11 games, tongues were wagging that Garvin was a goner. In fact, before the next match, Norris and Harkness told him he was dismissed. But then they had the nerve to ask him for a favor—would he coach the club that evening anyway? The problem was that the new coach was going to be Alex Delvecchio, but he hadn't had time to file his retirement papers. Since the NHL had recently passed a new bylaw that forbade any team from employing a playing coach, they needed a bench boss for the evening.

Unbelievably, Garvin agreed, but as the game wore on and the Wings were motoring toward another loss, Garvin decided he'd seen, done, and had enough. He simply left the bench, went to the dressing room, grabbed his coat, and left the building, leaving the rudderless Wings without a coach behind the bench. There was one sliver of silver lining for Mr. Garvin. Since Delvecchio had already officially been appointed as the new coach, the loss went on his record. He became the first NHL coach to lose a game before his coaching career had even started.

The First Finn

The first European-trained player—and first Finnish player—to be selected in the NHL Amateur Draft was Tommi Salmelainen, selected 66th overall by St. Louis in 1969. Salmelainen played the 1969–70 season with Kansas City of the CHL (22 points in 62 games) before returning to Finland to rejoin the Helsinki IFK club. In 1974, the Winnipeg Jets of the WHA signed their first two Finnish-trained players—Heikki Riihiranta and Veli-Pekka Ketola. The following season the Jets held their training camp in Finland and the influx of European talent increased. Pekka Rautakallio, who was signed by Atlanta as a free agent in June 1979, was the first Finn to play in the NHL.

Dave Reece gave up 11 goals, including six to Toronto's Darryl Sittler, in his final NHL appearance on February 7, 1976.

Reece's Pieces

When there's still an offensive record in the books that Wayne Gretzky and Mario Lemieux failed to break, you know it has legs. One mark that slipped through their collective grasp was Darryl Sittler's 10-point night against the Boston Bruins on February 7, 1976. The victim of Sittler's onslaught was a 27-year-old rookie named Dave Reece who was playing in his 14th—and final—NHL game on that dreadful evening at Maple Leaf Gardens.

But let's adjust our sets and deliver some credit to the shell-shocked freshman. Earlier in the week, Gerry Cheevers had bounced out of his contract with Cleveland of the WHA and was finally back in the Bruins fold. Incumbent Gilles Gilbert was still in the picture, so Reece went

Dave Reece

Hockey Stories On and Off the Ice

NHL President Clarence Campbell presented Darryl Sittler with a silver tea service to mark his 10-point night.

into that fateful game against the Maple Leafs knowing full well that his brief run at NHL stardom was coming to a close. In fact, Cheevers was dressed and on the bench for that evening in Toronto, but coach Don Cherry was saving him for the Bruins' next game, which was a Sunday evening encounter with Detroit back home in Boston. As he watched poor Reece fall victim to the Sittler surge, you can be sure Grapes was sour. After the game, which the Bruins lost 11–4, Reece was placed on the waiver wire and eventually assigned to the AHL's Springfield Indians. Some snide reporter made the comment that Reece attempted suicide that night by jumping onto the subway tracks in downtown Toronto, but the train went right through his legs.

Had Mr. Cherry not been "saving" Cheevers for his hometown return in Boston the following night—a triumphant 7–0 whitewashing of the Red Wings, by the way—Reece's lifetime statistics would have read: 13 games played, 7 wins, 4 losses, 2 ties, 2 shutouts, and a respectable 2.68 goals-against average. Of course, Sittler probably wouldn't have entered the record books and Dave Reece would have been just another forgotten footnote in NHL history.

Ironically, the first professional player to record 10 points in a game also had a Maple Leaf connection. Jim Harrison, who appeared in 175 games for Toronto between 1969–70 and 1971–72 before jumping to the WHA's Alberta Oilers, recorded 3 goals and 7 assists in an 11–3 victory over the New York Raiders on January 30, 1973.

Ottawa's Aberdeen Pavilion played host to the famed Silver Seven hockey club. The Seven successfully defended the Stanley Cup here in 1904.

GLORIOUS STORIES OF LORD STANLEY'S VENERABLE MUG

Mugging the Mug

In 1905, the Ottawa Silver Seven, obviously under the influence of some sweet champagne, felt it necessary to see if one of them could kick the Cup into Ottawa's Rideau Canal. One of the soused Seven lined up the silverware and gave it a boot, drop-kick style. In a true test of his accuracy and distance, the Cup landed on target, in the canal. With that established, the boys went on their merry way, and the Cup stayed in the canal until the next day, when sober heads prevailed and Lord Stanley's mug was rescued. It was then placed in the capable hands of Harry Smith, a member of the famed Silver Seven.

Where's Harry?

The Montreal Wanderers won the Cup in 1906, but when the players asked to see their prize, the Cup was nowhere to be found. Finally, someone remembered that Harry Smith had been given the mug to keep safe and sound. After a quick search of the Smith household, the Cup was retrieved and presented to the victorious Wanderers.

Planting Stanley's Seeds

The injustices of the Cup continued in 1907. The Wanderers quickly forgot the valuable lesson of the previous year and left the chalice at the home of the photographer they had hired to document their trophy win. A young fellow happened by and grabbed the trophy, hoping to extract a small ransom for its return. However, when no one was interested in meeting his demands, he returned it to the photographer's home. It was there that an astute lady-of-the-manor decided it would make a wonderful flower pot, and it served that purpose for a few months until the Wanderers brass remembered where it was and rescued Mr. Stanley's chalice from its earthly grave.

Mug on the Mantel

Upon returning home from the West Coast fresh from their surprising Stanley Cup victory in 1923, sophomore Senator Frank "King" Clancy asked the Ottawa executives if he could bring the Cup home to show his father, who was a well-known amateur athlete and the original "King."

The following season, NHL president Frank Calder asked the Senators to return the Stanley Cup, but they couldn't find it. It was then that that Clancy admitted it was still at his home, sitting on his mantelpiece.

The Champagne Wasn't Flat

After capturing the Stanley Cup title in 1924, the Montreal Canadiens wanted to celebrate in style by swilling champagne from the silver mug. The entire team stuffed themselves and their new piece of treasured silverware into Leo Dandurand's car and headed to their owner's home to belt back the bubbly. As fate would have it, they suffered a flat tire along the way. The lads bolted from the car, leaving Lord Stanley on the curb while they tended to the flat. They arrived at Dandurand's and prepared to serve the victory wine but discovered they'd left the Holy Grail sitting on the streets of Montreal. Back into the car they rumbled and motored back to where they had changed the flat. It was there that they found the Cup, perched proud as could be on a snowbank near the sidewalk.

Pilfering the Prize

Since the Montreal incident, the Stanley Cup has been given much better care, but it found itself in danger once again when the Chicago Blackhawks had the nerve to pluck the Cup from the grasp of the Montreal Canadiens, who had won it five times in succession. With the Habs losing in the semifinals to the Hawks, a die-hard Habs' fan hatched a plan to save the silverware from falling into the hands of the opposition. Our dedicated Montreal fan slipped into the lobby of the Chicago Stadium, where the trophy was being displayed in a glass case. He broke open the case, grabbed Lord Stanley, and made a beeline for freedom. However, he was quickly caught and the mug was rescued. His only excuse was that he couldn't stand seeing the Windy City win the coveted silverware.

Back Room Politics

After the Toronto Maple Leafs won the Cup in 1962, the original bowl and collar were retired to the Hockey Hall of Fame, where they were placed on display. In January 1970, the collar was stolen from the hall and it remained missing for several years, before an anonymous phone call told police to check the back room of a Toronto cleaning store for a very important piece of history. The police weren't sure what they would find, but there, wrapped like a Christmas present, was the original collar of the Stanley Cup, recovered after seven years in hibernation.

Not the Sharpest Knives in the Drawer

The current version of Lord Stanley's Cup was almost stolen again in 1977, but a keen-eyed employee of the Hockey Hall of Fame thwarted the attempt. Seven men, carrying a large gym bag and some suspicious tools were seen hovering near the Cup. When they were spotted, they dashed outside, only to be met by members of the city constabulary. In the would-be bandit's car, police found a series of photos detailing the floorplan of the Hall of Fame and the rest of the necessary equipment to pull off the job. Caught red-handed and red-faced, the lads were shipped off to jail without the Holy Grail.

Last Minute of Play

When *Slap Shot* played in Japan the working title translation was *The Roughhouse Hockey Players Who Curse a Lot and Play Dirty.*

The thing is I've only been here for about a year. It was probably my first game here. I remember how small it was compared to the other rinks. I liked walking in the lobby and looking at all the pictures on the walls. I grew up in Quebec City, so I didn't really didn't know about the Toronto tradition and history. I remember coming in here and looking at the banners and saying: "Wow! They've won a lot of Cups."

Former Leafs defender Sylvain Cote

Sometimes the team with the talent doesn't win it, because the other team wants to win it with their heart. That year we were first in the league, won the President's Trophy, had the best goals-against-average, went into the playoffs a little cocky and it ended up biting us in the butt.

Jeremy Roenick

All the records were gone. So I figured here's one record I can get.
Robert Dirk, after being assessed the Mighty Ducks of Anaheim's first ever instigator penalty

I'd trade Larry Murphy for a shaved monkey who could skate and a bucket of pucks.

Angry Toronto Maple Leafs fan

Jim Craig, gold medal hero in Lake Placid, played a total of 30 NHL games. He joined the Atlanta Flames after the Olympics in 1980 and played 23 games for Boston in 1980–81. His final three NHL games were with Minnesota in 1983–84.

The "Other" Paul Henderson

How often do Americans think about Jim Craig? How many Americans even remember who Jim Craig is? In 1980, that question was moot, because Jim Craig was a folk hero along the lines of Jesse James, Will Sutton, and Pretty Boy Floyd. What did Mr. Craig have in common with those three fugitives from justice? Well, they all committed highway robbery, but Craig did it legally, off the highway and on the ice.

When Paul Henderson scored his infamous goal that saved the state of Canadian hockey, he wasn't thinking about his country, his teammates, or the game. He was thinking of his father, the man who drove him to absurd levels so he could be the best he could be. Henderson's

Jim Craig

father was no longer alive when his son slipped a rebound past Vladislav Tretiak with only 34 seconds remaining in game eight of the "Series of the Century." But Paul's every thought was of the man who nurtured and sustained his dream of seeing his son play in the NHL.

It's fair to say that if you walked down any street in Canada and mentioned Paul Henderson's name to anyone over the age of 20, eight out of ten would be able to tell you who he was and what he did, whether they were sports fans or not. That's probably not true with Americans and Jim Craig.

Jim Craig was the goaltender of the 1980 USA Olympic hockey team that defeated the Soviet Union's Big Red Machine, virtually the same team that had embarrassed a team of NHL superstars by shellacking them 6–0 in the final game of a best-of-three tournament held during the 1978–79 NHL All-Star break. One year later, at the 1980 Winter Olympic Games, a team of U.S. college and university players, each of them true amateurs and all of them under the age of 24, defeated the USSR and then downed Finland to win the gold medal.

Jim Craig played a major role in that victory. Virtually unknown before his larcenous performance in Lake Placid, Craig was undrafted, sported a lid of curly locks, a scruffy look, and had a heart of gold. He stoned the Russians, finished off the Finns, and canceled the Canadians with a goaltending performance that can only be described as miraculous. Ask Al Michaels, the ABC TV commentator whose "Do you believe in miracles?" made him a media superstar. After the final gold medal–winning victory over Finland, Craig draped himself with an American flag and immediately went searching for his parents in the crowd. Like Henderson's, Craig's first thoughts were of family. The picture of this sweat-drenched goaltender wrapped in his nation's flag, longingly searching to share his glory with his parents, is one of the most enduring images ever featured on the cover of *Sports Illustrated* magazine.

Well, despite that unreal experience, the name Jim Craig has quietly disappeared into the "where-are-they-now" files. Perhaps it's because he never could translate that success to the professional game, or maybe it's just that when you've reached the pinnacle, where is there left to go? Jim Craig doesn't care. He's content in his memories.

"The nice part is that people seem to be happy when they talk to me about it. Everywhere I go, people tell me where they were, what they were doing, and how proud they were," he said recently; "it's so great not to have any of the pressure of trying to live up to something that was in the past."

Live on, Jim. Your place in hockey history is secure.

Lindsay Carson

Taking the Socks Out of Hockey

The basic components of a hockey uniform consist of a matching jersey, short pants and stockings. While each component has undergone extensive evolution, this look remained unchanged from the late 1890s until the 1970s when a new product called "Cooperalls" was introduced. Cooperalls consisted of a close fitting padded elastic undergarment and one-piece long nylon pants. Advantages claimed for the Cooperall system included that the undergarment kept the padding in place where it would better protect the player and that the pants were quick to put on and more durable than knit stockings.

Popular in youth and recreational hockey, the long-pants look was adopted by the Ontario Major Junior Hockey league in the late 1970s. It jumped to the NHL when the Philadelphia Flyers donned nylon in 1981–82. They were joined by the Hartford Whalers the following season. The new uniform style garnered mixed reviews. Some goalies felt it was hard to see the puck against the black legs of the Flyers' pants. Some players felt that they were too hot and many fans felt that the new uniforms just didn't look like hockey. The NHL deliberated and in the end opted for a traditional look, passing legislation that required short pants and home and away socks beginning with the 1983–84 season.

Hockey Hair

A popular beer commercial in Canada extols the virtues of the Great White North. Among the items singled out for praise are "your hockey hair" and "your long underwear." Hockey hair is not restricted to Canada but is an international condition that stems

John Garrett

Jocelyn Guevremont

Reggie Leach

Greg Malone

Dennis Maruk

Blair Chapman

Bernie Lukowich

Bobby Clarke

Paul Coffey

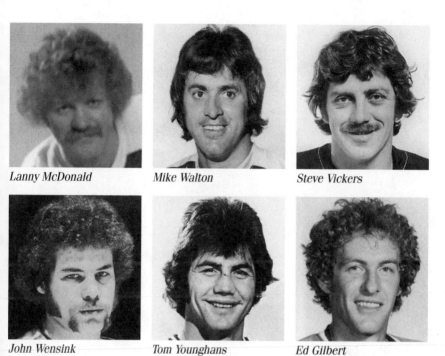

Lanny McDonald

Mike Walton

Steve Vickers

John Wensink

Tom Younghans

Ed Gilbert

from changing fashions, frequent showers, and, in the last few decades, the wearing of a helmet on the ice. Prime time for hockey hairstyles was the 1970s, when bangs, sideburns, big moustaches, and loads of locks were all in vogue. Here's a gallery of NHL shaggy dogs from that era.